A Short Historical Account of the Degrees in Music at Oxford and Cambridge

With a Chronological List of Graduates in that Faculty from the Year 1463

C. F. ABDY WILLIAMS

CAMBRIDGE UNIVERSITY PRESS

Cambridge, New York, Melbourne, Madrid, Cape Town, Singapore,
São Paolo, Delhi, Dubai, Tokyo

Published in the United States of America by Cambridge University Press, New York

www.cambridge.org
Information on this title: www.cambridge.org/9781108001847

© in this compilation Cambridge University Press 2009

This edition first published 1893
This digitally printed version 2009

ISBN 978-1-108-00184-7 Paperback

This book reproduces the text of the original edition. The content and language reflect the beliefs, practices and terminology of their time, and have not been updated.

Cambridge University Press wishes to make clear that the book, unless originally published by Cambridge, is not being republished by, in association or collaboration with, or with the endorsement or approval of, the original publisher or its successors in title.

A SHORT HISTORICAL ACCOUNT

OF THE

DEGREES IN MUSIC

AT

OXFORD AND CAMBRIDGE

WITH A CHRONOLOGICAL LIST OF GRADUATES IN THAT FACULTY FROM THE YEAR 1463

BY

C. F. ABDY WILLIAMS.

LONDON & NEW YORK
NOVELLO, EWER AND CO.

PREFACE.

THE attention which has of late years been given by our Universities to the cultivation of music, and the endeavour to again make the degrees of Doctor and Bachelor in that faculty of substantial value, as marks of real musical erudition and culture on the part of the holder, as was formerly the case, have induced me to try and investigate the early history of these degrees, which are peculiar to the English Universities, and are practically unknown abroad. My researches have led me to the conclusion that they arose at a time when English music was in a very advanced stage of development, in comparison with that of the Continent, and English musicians in consequence took a high rank, not only among contemporary musicians, but among the learned men of the day; and that our Universities gave degrees of an honorary nature, without requiring any examination or exercise, to eminent English musicians as marks of honour and esteem, rather than as mere " licences to teach." But in course of time, when less eminent musicians began to supplicate for these degrees, the Universities required some testimony as to the fitness of the applicant, and hence arose the necessity for the candidate to show that he had studied for a certain number of years; and in return for the favour of granting the degree a composition was demanded, to be performed before the University, as an addition to the ceremonies at " Act time"; and this became the exercise. How far I have succeeded in establishing this theory must be left to the reader to judge; in no other way can I account for the origin of degrees in music.

This is not the first "History of Musical Degrees," for in 1752 Johann Oelrichs, a Doctor of Law, published at Berlin a short " Historische Nachricht von den Academischen Würden in der Musik," chiefly dealing with English musical degrees and graduates. He says in Chapter iii.: "Nowhere has music received greater honour than in England, where, in London, Cambridge, and Oxford, not only has there been for a long time a special public teacher of music, . . . but from ancient times

England has given academical dignities in this art. It must not be thought, however, that a Doctor of Music is of little account, and the degree an empty title, or that it is easy to become such a Doctor. This degree is, on the contrary, far more difficult to attain than the highest honours in the chief faculties in German and other Universities. A Doctor in Music in England is a person of great importance, and takes rank, with the Doctors in other faculties, above the ordinary esquire, or gentleman entitled to bear arms, and both he and the Bachelor of Music wear special robes of honour." Oelrichs' little book goes on to describe the statutory requirements for graduating in music, and he is evidently much struck with their searching and arduous nature. He afterwards discusses the question of Allibond's degree—*i.e.*, whether it was that of "Master in Music"—but comes to the conclusion that it was "Master in Arts." After this there is an alphabetical list of some of the more important English Doctors, and lists of the Gresham, Heather, and Cambridge Professors of Music; and the book concludes with a short account of what each foreign University does in the way of teaching music. The book is interesting as showing something of the view that obtained abroad in the last century on English musical degrees; but its material is mostly gathered from Wood, and the author had evidently not visited the English Universities.

I have traced the course of the degrees from the earliest time they are mentioned, to the present day, when the tendency becomes more and more marked to place music on a level in every respect with the other faculties. I have in all cases given references to the authorities for my statements, and wish here to offer my best thanks for assistance and information given me by Professor S. S. Laurie, of Edinburgh University; the Rev. H. Rashdall, of Hertford College, Oxford; Dr. C. Harford Lloyd; Mr. H. B. Briggs, the Hon. Secretary of the Plainsong and Mediæval Music Society; Mr. Charles Sayle; Mr. A. Hughes-Hughes; the Rev. J. Mee, Mus. Doc.; Mr. George Parker, the Clerk of the Schools, Oxford; and especially to Mr. J. W. Clark, the Registrary of Cambridge University, to whom I am indebted for most valuable assistance with regard to the early Cambridge Graces.

The edition of Hawkins' History referred to is that published by Novello, in three volumes, in 1853, the pagination of which is continuous.

C. F. A. W.

December, 1893.

CAMBRIDGE LIBRARY COLLECTION
Books of enduring scholarly value

Music
The systematic academic study of music gave rise to works of description, analysis and criticism, by composers and performers, philosophers and anthropologists, historians and teachers, and by a new kind of scholar - the musicologist. This series makes available a range of significant works encompassing all aspects of the developing discipline.

A Short Historical Account of the Degrees in Music at Oxford and Cambridge
C. F. Abdy Williams (1855-1923), a noted music scholar, traced the history of the discipline at Oxford and Cambridge from the fifteenth century to the late Victorian period in this 1894 book. He discusses the earliest records of degrees in the subject, the establishment of professorships, the requirements for degrees and the ceremonies associated with their conferral. He provides biographical information for graduates from as early as 1463, noting that English music of this early period was in a very advanced stage compared to that of the rest of Europe. He also includes in an appendix the names of those persons who are mentioned as graduates but whose names do not appear in the university records. His book reveals the importance attached to the cultivation of music at the ancient British universities and the prestige attached to their scholars over several centuries.

Cambridge University Press has long been a pioneer in the reissuing of out-of-print titles from its own backlist, producing digital reprints of books that are still sought after by scholars and students but could not be reprinted economically using traditional technology. The Cambridge Library Collection extends this activity to a wider range of books which are still of importance to researchers and professionals, either for the source material they contain, or as landmarks in the history of their academic discipline.

Drawing from the world-renowned collections in the Cambridge University Library, and guided by the advice of experts in each subject area, Cambridge University Press is using state-of-the-art scanning machines in its own Printing House to capture the content of each book selected for inclusion. The files are processed to give a consistently clear, crisp image, and the books finished to the high quality standard for which the Press is recognised around the world. The latest print-on-demand technology ensures that the books will remain available indefinitely, and that orders for single or multiple copies can quickly be supplied.

The Cambridge Library Collection will bring back to life books of enduring scholarly value (including out-of-copyright works originally issued by other publishers) across a wide range of disciplines in the humanities and social sciences and in science and technology.

CONTENTS.

Chapter I.
THE ORIGIN OF ACADEMICAL DEGREES IN GENERAL ... PAGE 7

Chapter II.
THE EARLIEST RECORDS OF DEGREES IN MUSIC ... 13

Chapter III.
EARLY MUSICAL STUDY AT THE UNIVERSITIES.—BOETHIUS ... 20

Chapter IV.
THE MUSIC ACT, MUSIC SPEECH OR LECTURE, AND MUSIC SCHOOL ... 27

Chapter V.
THE ESTABLISHMENT OF PROFESSORS OF MUSIC AT THE UNIVERSITIES ... 34

Chapter VI.
DEVELOPMENT OF THE MODERN REQUIREMENTS FOR MUSICAL DEGREES ... 40

Chapter VII.
THE CULTIVATION OF MUSIC AT THE UNIVERSITIES ... 45

Chapter VIII.
ACADEMICAL DRESS.—DEGREE CEREMONIES, FEASTS.—AN EARLY EXAMINATION FOR THE B.A. DEGREE ... 57

Chapter IX.

OXFORD GRADUATES IN MUSIC, WITH BIO-
GRAPHICAL SKETCHES 64

Chapter X.

CAMBRIDGE GRADUATES IN MUSIC, WITH BIO-
GRAPHICAL SKETCHES 119

APPENDIX, CONTAINING ACCOUNTS OF THOSE
PERSONS WHO ARE MENTIONED IN HISTORY
AS GRADUATES, BUT WHOSE NAMES DO NOT
APPEAR IN THE UNIVERSITY RECORDS 152

SOME EARLY GRACES, &c., RELATING TO DEGREES
IN MUSIC 153

DEGREES IN MUSIC.

CHAPTER I.

THE ORIGIN OF ACADEMICAL DEGREES IN GENERAL.

ACADEMICAL Degrees, as we know them, appear to have originated at the University of Bologna, in the first half of the twelfth century, and were probably modelled on those given by Justinian* to the students of his academies at Rome, Constantinople, and Berytus.†

Bayle's account of their origin is as follows: " Irnerius, a German (also called Wernerius, and Guarnerius), Chancellor to the Emperor Lotharius, was the first who renewed the study and profession of Roman Law, after its interruption by the barbarians. He was Professor of Law at the University of Bologna,‡ and is said to have persuaded the Emperor to introduce into that University the creation of *Doctors*, the forms and ceremonies for which degree he arranged; and the first who were promoted to this honour were Bulgarus, Hugolinus, Martin, Pileus, and some others, who began to interpret and teach Roman Law.§ The degree of Doctor having thus been established at Bologna, soon spread to Salerno, where degrees were given in Medicine;‖ and

---

* Bulæus, " Hist. Univ. Pariensis," II., 255.
† Hoefer, " Nouvelle Biog. Générale," Tom. XXVII., p. 327.
‡ Bologna University was founded in A.D. 425, and incorporated A.D. 1119, and in the Middle Ages contained sometimes as many as 12,000 students.—Meyer, " Conversations-Lexicon," Ed. of 1845 and 1886.
§ Bayle, " Dict. Hist." Art. " Irnerius."
‖ The doctorate in medicine having been introduced at Salerno, was sometimes given in the eleventh, twelfth, and thirteenth centuries to women as well as men. Constantia Calenda and others received the degree (English Cyclopædia, " Salernitana Schola "). And at Bologna, Beltica Gozadina was made Doctor and Professor of Law (Itterus, " Diatriba de gradibus "). The Catalogue of Dublin Graduates also mentions several female Doctors of Canon and Civil Law and Professors of Medicine and Surgery at Bologna.

to Paris, where they were given in Theology as well as the other two faculties.

Bulæus gives the following account:—"Gratianus was the first collector and compiler of the Decretal Epistles, which he published, and dedicated to Pope Eugene III. (who reigned from 1145 to 1154). But since students had been applying themselves to civil law, Pope Eugene, fearing that canon law might fall into contempt, at the suggestion of Gratian devised certain academical degrees: the Baccalauriat, the Licentiate, and the Doctorate, that by means of these special titles he might induce students to study canon law and might make them eager to obtain the proposed privileges." Bulæus goes on to say that the greater number of authors acknowledge this to have been the origin of academical degrees, and assert that they were first instituted in the Academy of Bologna; and it is evident that Gratian modelled his degrees on those given by Justinian in civil law.*

Peter Lombard, the "Master of the Sentences," who had studied at Bologna, is said to have instituted, and been the first to receive, the degree of Doctor of Theology at the University of Paris, about 1151, whither he had been attracted by the fame of its professors.†

Another view of the matter, and the one most generally accepted now, is that the fame of the University of Paris having attracted a large number of students, it was found that many pretenders to learning soon appeared amongst them, and easily imposed upon a youthful and enthusiastic audience. Hence it became necessary as a protection, both to the students and their teachers, to grant licences to those who were properly qualified to teach, and to impose some test before doing so, out of which arose the system of examinations. The University Degree was, therefore, anciently simply a licence to teach, and in later times the holder not only had this right, but was held bound to exercise it.‡

The use of the word Master as the title of a degree seems to

---

* Bulæus, "Hist. Univ. Par.," II., p. 255.
† "Biog. Universelle," Vol. XXIV., p. 641; and Bul., II., 257.
‡ Mullinger, "The Univ. of Cambridge from the Earliest Times," I., 77. Laurie, "Rise and Constitution of English Universities." Hüber, "Die Eng. Universitäten," I., 44. Maxwell Lyte, "Hist. of Oxford," p. 237.

have arisen later than that of Doctor, although both titles were at one time used indiscriminately for the highest degree in any faculty.* Specht† says, however, that the name Master was applied, before the institution of the ceremony of conferring the Doctorate, to professors of all sciences, languages and arts.

The candidate for the degree of Master of Arts was required to have a thorough knowledge of the seven liberal arts called the Trivium and Quadrivium. Those contending for this degree had as their first " Act " to carry on a solemn disputation, *ad terminorum determinationes*, and, if successful, became Bachelors of Arts. Those who attempted this disputation and were unable to perform it, were called down, confused and ridiculed, as was a certain Trebatius, who had neglected his exercises, at Paris.‡ Besides the disputation, the candidate for the Mastership was obliged to fulfil certain conditions, such as that he should possess the proper books for his profession, should instruct others less learned than himself, and should practise disputing in the schools of the Masters, in order to render himself worthy of promotion.

The degree of Licentiate seems to be older than that of Master or Doctor, and was apparently originally given by the bishop or scholasticus of a diocese. It was a license to teach, and was conferred by the University of Paris on the candidate for the doctorate or mastership as soon as he was fit for it, in order to give him the right of imparting instruction to others. We find the word in 1246, when Matthew of Paris, *Licentiavit familiam.*§ But earlier than this, certain persons were sent out from Rome, licensed by the Pope or his Chancellor to teach, without having undergone the labour of disputing or frequenting the schools,‖ a practice which in 1229 gave rise to disturbances at Paris, for the Senate of that University would not accept as members those whose degrees had been thus given by the Pope; nor could the thunders of the Vatican compel them to do so. The custom was established by 1179, for we find the Lateran Council of that year

---

* In the Middle Ages we constantly meet with " *Magistri in Theologia* " and in Italy there were "*Doctores Artium.*" (Information from Rev. H. Rashdall.)
† " De honoribus." Wittenberg, 1631, p. 48.
‡ Bulæus, II., 677.
§ Bulæus, II., 681.
‖ Idem.

enacting that no price is to be demanded by a bishop for the license to teach.*

The derivation of the word Bachelor has been so variously given, that it would take too much space to quote here all the conjectures that have been made as to its origin. Spelman† says that a "Bacularius" is a person who is formally received into the number of those who are commencing the higher studies: hence is a beginner. In military matters, Bacularii or Knights Bachelors were those who, having passed through the stage of recruitship, were beginning their military career.

Other derivations are from "$\beta\alpha\kappa\eta\lambda o\varsigma$," foolish; "Bas Chevalier," a knight of the lowest rank; "Baculus," a staff; "Bucella," an allowance of provision; "Bacca-Laureus," the berry of a laurel or bay.‡ The degree of Bachelor of Arts was usually conferred after four years spent in the study of the Trivium, or three lower liberal arts, which consisted of grammar, rhetoric, and logic. It was the first degree conferred upon the candidate for the mastership, and having obtained it he was obliged to spend a further period of three years in the study of the four higher arts of the Quadrivium—namely, arithmetic, geometry, music, and astronomy.

The earliest notice we have of forms and ceremonies being prescribed for the conferring of University degrees, dates from 1231, in which year Gregory IX. seems to have introduced those for the degrees of Bachelor, Licentiate, and Master or Doctor, in the faculties of Arts, Medicine, Law, and Theology; for Renatus Choppinus prefixes to a bull of 1231 the words, "Apostolicum diploma de forma et modo decorandi academicis gradibus scholastici";§ and after this time frequent mention is made of Bachelors, Licentiates, and Masters of Theology and other faculties.

---

* Bul., II., 681 and 684. The right which still vests in the Archbishop of Canterbury of giving the degree of Doctor of Music, and demanding a fee of £63 (Grove's Dict., I., 452), is probably a remnant of the ancient custom here referred to. The Archbishop can also grant degrees in other faculties to eminent persons: and in 1671 we find Thomas Baker making a strong protest against the action of the Senate of Cambridge University, in creating a precedent for the admission of Lambeth Graduates to the privileges of the University by incorporation, on precisely the same grounds as those on which the Paris Senate objected to incorporating the Pope's Licentiates in 1229. (Baker MSS., Vol. XLII.)   † Gloss, 1687, p. 54.

‡ Hawkins, "Hist. Music," p. 292.   § Bulæus, II., 682 and 684.

In early times, nearly all knowledge and teaching were directed towards the one absorbing study of theology. "The seven liberal arts are the way," says Alcuin to his pupils, " in which you must learn to walk daily in your youth, till you are grown up, and prepared to dedicate yourselves to the highest tasks of Christian study." *

The advantages of these arts have been thus summed up. Grammar was of service for teaching how to read and transcribe the Scriptures, rhetoric and logic for explaining the Fathers and refuting adversaries, music was necessary for the proper performance of divine worship, arithmetic trained the mind to that regularity and order necessary for the study of theology, astronomy taught the contemplation of the heavenly bodies; while geometry, being only concerned with purely earthly things, was considered as the stepson of the liberal arts, and was not so much cultivated as the others.

In the Middle Ages, after a candidate for academical honours had prepared his mind by the studies of the Trivium and Quadrivium, and had received the Mastership in Arts, he was allowed to commence his studies for the Bachelorship and Doctorship of Theology (afterwards called Divinity), Law, or Medicine; and for this a further period of time was prescribed, in addition to the seven years spent in acquiring the Mastership of Arts.

The degree system soon spread over Western Europe, and its influence was naturally felt at the English Universities. Oxford was founded in 1249, and is called by Bulæus the eldest daughter of Paris; † and at Cambridge, which was founded in 1284, the customs were disposed after the manner of those of Paris. The title of Doctor seems to have come into use at Oxford later than that of Master, but after its introduction both titles were used, as on the Continent, for the highest degree in any faculty. Trevetti says, that in the year 1294 Edward I. sent Fre Huges de Malmecestre, *Master* of Divinity, to render his homage to the King of France; and Mathew Paris tells us that in 1267 the *Masters* of Oxford came to the Parliament.‡

Anthony Wood ("Annals," Vol. II., Book ii., p. 722) says

---

* Specht, " Geschichte des Unterricht-Wesens in Deutschland," 1885, p. 82.
† Bul., II., 544. See also Laurie, " Rise and Constitution of the Universities," p. 242.
‡ Spelman, " Gloss.," *Magister*, and Hüber, " Die Eng. Univ.," II., 192.

that in early times degrees were given at Oxford in the single liberal arts, such as grammar, rhetoric, poetry, and music; and Mr. Wise, in a letter quoted by Hawkins (p. 292), also takes this view, which he probably derived from Wood. But I have been able to find no direct evidence that such degrees were ever given at our Universities in any subject except grammar; and I shall show that degrees in music were originally so different from those in grammar, that they cannot be placed in the same category. The grammar degrees were of a very inferior nature, and conferred no privileges on the holder, who had, in fact, to pay a yearly sum to the University in return for being allowed to teach. The requirements for these degrees are fully laid down by statute from very early times. No residence was demanded before the conferring of the degree, but there were several rather elaborate examinations or disputations, and the Master in Grammar ranked with the Bachelor of Arts.

The last Oxford Bachelor of Grammar of which we have any mention was Thomas Ashbroke, who graduated on July 10, 1568,* and the last Cambridge Master of Grammar took his degree in 1542. We get an insight into the requirements for these degrees at Oxford in 1511-12, when Edward Watson and Maurice Byrchynshaw were admitted "ad docendum in eadem facultate," the first, on condition of his composing, within a year, 100 poems in praise of the University, and a comedy; the second, on condition of his composing 100 poems on the nobility of the University.† Masters in Grammar, however, seem not always to have been forthcoming when required, for we find in 1455 that Robert Abdy (afterwards Master of Balliol), and Master Joyner, were appointed to act as "Magistri Grammaticales."‡

The Oxford graduates in grammar were originally masters of Grammar schools in the town; but they were bound to dispute at stated times with Masters of Arts,§ probably in order to prevent them from neglecting to keep up their knowledge of grammar, since their duties were only to prepare boys for the Bachelor's degree.

---

* Boase, "Registrum Univ. Ox.," page 269.
† Boase, "Registrum Univ. Ox.," page 298.
‡ Boase, "Registrum," 24.
§ Anstey, "Munimenta Academica," I., 86, from the Chancellor's and Proctors' Books of 1301.

CHAPTER II.

THE EARLIEST RECORDS OF DEGREES IN MUSIC.

IT is not known when these degrees were first conferred by Oxford and Cambridge, and they have never been given by foreign Universities.* Some foreign writers have considered that they originated in the practice of giving degrees in the single arts of the seven liberal studies; and there is a certain amount of reason for this view, for they were similar to the grammar degrees, in that no residence was required, and that they did not confer full membership of the University on the recipient.†

My own view is that they were considered more honourable than degrees in grammar, and that the Doctorate in Music was at first conferred only on musicians of eminence, and without examination. It is known that, in the Middle Ages, music took a very high rank in public estimation in England, and English musicians had considerable reputation abroad. MSS. have recently been found at Modena, Bologna, and among the capitular archives of Trent, dating from the latter part of the fifteenth century, which contain compositions by Dunstable, John Benet, Forest, Power, Stowe, and others, showing that the music of English composers was known and appreciated abroad. There is evidence, moreover, that Dunstable preceded Dufay and Binchois by some years, and that the early English School of music, the development of which was crushed by the general disturbance of all the arts of peace caused by

---

* Some foreign Universities have, however, given the degree of Mus. Doc. *without examination* in modern times, to eminent musicians, as in the case of Andreas Romberg, Spontini, Schneider, and the late Robert Franz, who was a Mus. Doc. of Halle. Mr. Rashdall informs me that there were *Magistri in Musica* in the thirteenth century at some Spanish Universities.

† This view originated with Wood, who says that graduates in grammar, rhetoric, poetry, and music were accounted the most inferior in the University because they had only applied themselves to a single art.—"Annals," Vol. II., Book ii., p. 723.

the Wars of the Roses, was flourishing before the rise of the Netherlands School.*

The earliest University statutes, while giving full particulars as to the requirements for the degree of Master of Grammar, are silent with regard to degrees in music. The earliest mention I have found of the latter in any statutes occurs in those given by Elizabeth to Cambridge in 1559, in which the lists of fees to be paid by a Bachelor and Inceptor† in Music are given; and the fees for Bachelors and Inceptors in Medicine are stated to be the same as for those degrees in music.‡

A few years later we meet with a curious decree of the Prefects, dated May 8, 1571, referring to Bachelors of Music amongst other graduates. It is to the effect that any student bathing, or washing, in the river or any pond in the County of Cambridge, shall be punished by public whipping by the Vice-Chancellor; and for the second offence he shall be expelled the University. If the delinquent is a Bachelor of Arts, he is to be put in the stocks for one day; and if he is a Master of Arts or Bachelor of Law, Medicine, or Music, or holds any higher degree, he shall be punished according to the judgment of the head of his college.§

---

* See Grove's Dict. IV., 619; "Dict. Nat. Biog.," Dunstable; letter to *Times* newspaper, February 21, 1893, from Mr. Barclay Squire. Ambros, Vol. III., p. 453, gives the following additional names of English composers of this school, and shows that they were very much esteemed in Italy: Gervasius de Anglia, Zacarias Anglicanus, Johannes Wylde; and there are two compositions in the Liceo at Bologna inscribed "de Anglia" and "Anglicanum." Hawkins quotes (p. 291) the following remark of Erasmus: "As nature has implanted self-love in the minds of all mortals, so she has disposed to every country and nation a certain tincture of the same affection. Hence it is that the English challenge the prerogative of having the most handsome women, *of being the most accomplished in the skill of music*, and of keeping the best tables."—*Erasmus*, "Moriæ encomium," Basle Ed., p. 101.

† The title Inceptor is applied to Doctors and Masters in any faculty immediately after taking their degree. It means a beginner, that is a person who is beginning his work as a Master or Doctor by a year's lecturing (Anstey's "Munimenta Acad.," Introd. p. xcii.). The statutes of Laud speak indiscriminately of the Inceptor and Doctor of Music.

‡ From "Statuta Acad. Cantab.," Ed. of 1785, p. 195, and the Baker MSS. The fees for the Bachelor are as follows: Vicecancellario, 2s.; præsentatori (the graduate who presents the candidate), 2s.; procuratoribus (proctors), 2s.; pro communa (common chest), 20d.; registro (registrar), 4d.; pulsatori (bell ringer), 12d.; bedellis pro collectis (bedells), 4s. 8d.; pro prandiis (feasts), 18d.; pro chirothecis (gloves), 18d.; pro introitu (entrance money), 6s. 8d.; pro visitatione, 6s. 8d. The doctor paid the same items at a higher rate, his total amounting to 51s. 8d. In 1803 the expenses of taking the degree of Mus. Bac. had increased to £70 (*Camb. Univ. Calendar*).

§ "Statuta Acad. Cant.," p. 454.

THE EARLIEST RECORDS OF DEGREES IN MUSIC. 15

It is significant that this notice, which, after the statutes of 1559, is the earliest record of any regulations regarding graduates in music, seems to rank the Bachelor in Music with the Master of Arts, and the Bachelor of Law and Medicine.

The Oxford statutes of 1356 prescribe for four faculties—Arts, Theology, Law, and Medicine. Music is not reckoned among the faculties.* Grammar was called a faculty before music, and it seems as if, in the early graces relating to musical degrees, every effort was made to avoid applying the word faculty to Music.† New regulations appear to have been made for each fresh candidate for a degree in music, and this could probably easily be done, since so few persons applied for these degrees.

The first Doctor of Music of whom there is any mention is Saint Just or Saintwix, who was made Master or Warden of King's Hall,‡ Cambridge, in 1463, by Edward IV., whose chaplain he was. In the document granting him this appointment he is called "Magister," from which we may reasonably infer that he had passed through the ordinary University course, and taken the M.A. degree before becoming a Doctor of Music.§ Although he is the first Doctor of Music of whom there is any record, there is nothing to show that the degree was not conferred before this time. The inference is that it was already well established, at Cambridge, at all events.

The next mention of the Doctorate in Music we meet with is in connection with Henry Habyngton or Abyngdon, who took his Bachelor's degree in 1463, and whose grace was granted that he might proceed to the Doctorate on condition of his residing in Cambridge one year, but whether he did so, does not appear.|| He is said to have been pre-eminent as a singer and organist.¶

Soon afterwards we hear of John Hamboys, or Hanboys, who flourished about 1470, a person who was very eminent not only in

---

* Cotton MSS., Claud., D. viii.
† *See* Graces in Appendix—C, E, F, G, H, I, J, &c. It is, however, used in K. Graces referring to grammar almost invariably use the expression "eadem facultate." The word faculty means a body of persons teaching and studying the same subject (Du Cange). Music, except to the extent required for the M.A. degree, was not taught and studied in the Universities; hence it was not one of their faculties, and only came to be considered one when they examined candidates for degrees.
‡ Afterwards absorbed into Trinity College by Henry VIII. Hawkins confuses it with King's College.
§ *See* Appendix D. || *See* Appendix C. ¶ Grove's Dict., 1, 6.

music, but in other arts, and especially in Latin and mathematics. Holinshed describes him as "an excellent musician, and for his notable cunning therein made Doctor of Music."* Pits † does not mention that he was made a Doctor of Music, but is eloquent on his musical attainments, saying that he compared with the best musicians of his time. Bale ‡ says that he was made Doctor "by common suffrage," being certainly the most celebrated musician of his time in England. It is not known which University thus honoured him, and it is just possible that Bale's words "Communi suffragio" may mean that he did not graduate at either, but that the title was conferred on him by the *vox populi*.

After Hamboys we find Robert Cooper, or Cowpar, a Mus. Bac. of Cambridge, who proceeds Doctor there in 1502,§ and is mentioned by Morley among famous English musicians. Like Saintwix, he is also styled "Magister." In the same year, Robert Fairfax, or Fayrfax, or Ferfax, was admitted Mus. Doc. at Cambridge.‖ He was a very eminent musician, and was Organist of St. Alban's Abbey, which then contained the finest organ in England.¶ He is the first Oxford Doctor in Music of whom there is any record, having incorporated there in 1511,** though there is nothing to show that Oxford never made Doctors of Music previously to this.

We now reach the period when conditions began to be imposed upon candidates for the Degree of Mus. Doc. In 1515 we find that Robert Perrot's request for this degree at Oxford was granted on condition of his composing a mass and one song ; †† and in 1531 John Guinneth was required to compose a mass. The latter tried hard to get the degree given him on his reputation as a composer, and the University finally granted it without requiring the mass, but made him pay 20d. for the favour.‡‡ He is mentioned among famous English musicians by Morley, and both he and Perrot were of reputation as composers. The only other persons upon whom the degree of Mus. Doc. was

---

* "Chronicles," III., 710, Ed. of 1587. † Vol. I., 662, Ed. 1619.
‡ "Scriptorum Catalogus," 617. § App. H.
‖ Burney wrongly gives the date as 1511, in which year he incorporated at Oxford.
¶ "Dict. Nat. Biog." "Fairfax." ** Foster, "Alumni Ox."
†† Wood, "Fasti Oxonienses." ‡‡ *See* p. 68.

conferred in the sixteenth century, as far as is known, were Fryvill, at Cambridge, in 1504; Christopher Tye, at Cambridge, in 1545 (incorporated at Oxford, 1548); John Bull, at Cambridge, about 1591 (incorporated at Oxford, 1592); and Stevenson, at Oxford, 1596.

In the earliest times, the candidate for the Doctorate was under no necessity at either University of having previously become a Bachelor in Music; but when Oxford began to make statutory provisions for musical degrees, the candidate was required not only to have graduated as a Bachelor before proceeding Doctor, but a period of five years was fixed by Laud's statutes as the minimum of time which must elapse between taking the two degrees. But in certain cases the two degrees might be " accumulated " on the same day, when, for instance, the candidate was already a man of reputation. At Cambridge, on the other hand, there was no necessity until the year 1889 for a candidate for the Doctorate to have previously taken the Bachelor's degree, and, until quite recently, persons were created Mus. Doc. without having done so.*

Doctors in Music were in no way connected with the Universities as teachers, and cannot be placed in the same category with Masters of Grammar. The title of Doctor has for many centuries been considered more honourable than that of Master, and those musicians on whom it was conferred were men of eminence† at a time when music ranked as a very honourable profession.

With regard to the Bachelor of Music, I believe the case was different. Although both degrees in music were very rarely given in comparison with those in the other faculties, yet a considerably larger number of persons received the lower than the higher degree, and these, though often, were by no means always, eminent musicians. The degree conferred the

---

* A. Wall's " Cambridge Ceremonies," 1798, says that a Doctor in Music " is not obliged to be a Bachelor before he is a Doctor," and in the " Excerpta Statutis Acad. Cant.," published in 1732, a list of fees is given for Inceptors in Music, Medicine, and Law who have not previously taken the Baccalauriat.

† I have been able to find no particulars, however, of Humfrey Fryvill, or Frevill, who graduated Mus. Doc. at Cambridge in 1504. He was possibly a member of a family of that name which had been for many generations seated at Little Shelford, near Cambridge. His name is not mentioned by Morley, and apparently none of his compositions are extant.

right of reading and lecturing on the books of Boethius at Oxford, and of lecturing on the "science" of music at Cambridge.* Henry Habyngton, the first Bachelor of Music we hear of, seems to have taken this degree as a preliminary step to that of Mus. Doc., though he was under no necessity to do so. He was undoubtedly eminent as a musician.

Baker, in his lists of Cambridge graduates, while he is careful to give the names of all those who graduated as Doctors of Music, does not always consider it worth while to give those of the Bachelors, merely mentioning the number of persons proceeding Mus. Bac. in any particular year. The Oxford lists are more imperfect than those of Cambridge, and the first definite date we get for the degree of Mus. Bac. is 1504, in which year Henry Parker, of Magdalen Hall, took this degree. That Oxford made Bachelors of Music before this, however, is clear, for Robert Wydow incorporated at Cambridge in 1502 as a Mus. Bac. of Oxford : and since Wood's " Fasti " begins with 1500 and does not mention him, it is tolerably certain that he must have graduated at Oxford before that date. Wood, being so great a lover of music, was careful to mention as far as possible the names and position of all graduates in music, and seems anxious to show that the majority of them were important members of their profession.

Of musical studies at the Universities in the Middle Ages, I shall speak in the next chapter. The requirements for the degree of Mus. Bac. seem to have been vague, and probably were only announced to the candidate on the day that the grace was granted allowing him to take his degree.† At first apparently no examination was required, and no composition, for either degree. All that the candidate had to do was to state in his supplication that he had studied and practised music for a certain time, usually seven years. Thus H. Fryvill spent two years in Cambridge, and five elsewhere, and his grace was granted. Lessy's time of study is not mentioned. Beryderyke, in 1519, however, was not allowed his degree so easily. He had spent one year in Cambridge in " speculation " on music, and five elsewhere in practice and

---

* Appendix, I. J.
† Graduates in music were not required to have been matriculated until 1870 at Oxford and 1881 at Cambridge. Stat. Univ. Ox., 1883, p. 112, and Camb. Univ. Calendar, 1881.

teaching; but was required to compose a mass.* John Watkins and John Firtun were each required to compose a mass and antiphon.† Christopher Tye‡ was required to compose a mass for his Bachelor's degree, "to be sung either shortly after the Comitia, or on the day on which the accession of the most serene Prince (Henry VIII.) shall be observed; or at least to show some specimen of his erudition in the Comitia." For the Doctorate, a mass was demanded of him, to be sung at the Comitia. In Elizabeth's reign a communion service was required to be composed and performed at St. Mary's, in place of the mass.§

The same conditions seem to have prevailed at Oxford. Wood mentions no requirements as having been imposed on the earlier applicants for degrees in music. The first from whom a composition was demanded seems to have been John Wendon, who, in 1509, was required to compose a mass to be sung at the Act following. In 1515 Robert Perrot was required to compose a mass and one song, and in 1516 John Draper's "request was granted with one or two conditions." No mention of a disputation, such as was required for all other degrees, occurs until 1622, when N. Giles took his Doctor's degree (*see* page 70), but even then the questions, being merely a matter of form, were omitted. Regular examinations were not instituted till a much later date.

---

* Appendix, K.   † Appendix, I. J.
‡ Appendix, L. M.   § Appendix, N.

CHAPTER III.

EARLY MUSICAL STUDY AT THE UNIVERSITIES.—BOETHIUS.

Music formed an important element in Mediæval education, whether it was studied with a view to the taking of a musical degree or not. By the Oxford Statutes of 1431 arithmetic and music were each to be studied for one year, in addition to the other subjects necessary for the degree of Master of Arts.* Astronomy and geometry are to be studied only two terms each, being evidently considered of inferior value to arithmetic and music. The books of Boethius were required for the degree of Bachelor in Music, as well as for that of M.A., but apparently the graduate in music was expected to have a larger knowledge of them than the M.A., and was permitted to lecture on any of them. But all clerks were expected to " bene con, bene can, and bene le "—*i.e.*, "construe well, sing well, and read well ";—and we have ample evidence that instruction in singing was provided for all the junior members of the Universities. On the fifth Thursday in Lent all determiners were examined in " Songe and wryhtynge." The statutes of Clare Hall, which was founded 1359, require that the sizars shall be represented by ten docile, proper, and respectable youths, who are to be educated in singing, grammar, and logic ; and that every Sunday and Holy-Day the fellows and sizars are to attend High Mass and sing at it.†
At Oxford, every master was, by the statutes of 1356, expected to attend High Mass at St. Mary's Church at the commencement and conclusion of every academical year,‡ and provision was made for suitable vestments and proper behaviour on their part. Candidates for scholarships at Winchester and New College,

---

* Of studies necessary before inception, 1431: " Arithmeticam per terminum anni, videlicet Boethii. Musicam per terminum anni, videlicet Boethii." Anstey, " Munimenta Academica," Vol. I., p. 286.
† Heywood, "Early Cambridge Statutes," Part ii., pp 138, 139.
‡ Cotton MSS., Statutes of 1356.

Oxford, were examined in reading, Latin, grammar, and plain chant.* For the degree of Bachelor in Music, no knowledge of music, except singing, and the science as represented by Boethius, appears to have been required in early times. Not till the beginning of the sixteenth century do we hear of compositions being demanded; and it is probable that even then, the original object in requiring them was, that there should be a Music "Act" at the ceremony of conferring degrees, in order to add to its solemnity. The study of Boethius formed a large portion of the conditions for the degree of Bachelor in Music, down to a comparatively late period. A survival of this is seen in the form of supplication in use at Oxford down to 1856, which ran as follows :—"A. B. ... supplicates, that having performed all the requirements of the statutes, he may be admitted to lecture in any book of Boethius."† These words disappear in the collection of statutes published in 1883; ‡ hence they were done away with as lately as between 1856 and 1883. But, true to tradition, both the Universities have revived somewhat of the old scholastic spirit in this respect, by requiring candidates for musical degrees to be examined in acoustics, which subject is merely a modernised and simplified form of the matter treated by Boethius.

Since it may be of interest to the modern musical graduate to know something of the nature of those "musical books" which his predecessors had to spend so much time in studying, I will conclude this chapter with a short account of Boethius and his writings on music.

Anitius Manlius Torquatus Severinus Boethius was of an ancient Roman family, members of which had been Senators and Consuls. He was born at Rome between A.D. 470 and 475, during the time that Odoacer, King of the Herulians, reigned in Italy. Boethius was sent to Athens for his education, on the completion of which, he returned to Rome, where he soon distinguished himself for his learning and virtue, and was advanced in course of time to the Consulate. He was deeply versed in theology, mathematics, ethics, and logic, and many of his works are still extant.

---

* Maxwell-Lyte, "History of Oxford," p. 190.
† "Statuta Univ. Oxon.," 1857, p. 88.
‡ "Statuta Univ. Oxon.," 1883, p. 135.

In 493 Theodoric the Goth, having murdered Odoacer, became King of Italy, and ruled for thirty-three years with great prudence and moderation, and Boethius became his most important minister. Theodoric, however, was an Arian; and Justin, Emperor of Constantinople, and Horsmida, Bishop of Rome, having published an edict against Arianism, three enemies of Boethius took advantage of this occasion to falsely accuse him of plotting against Theodoric. He was in consequence thrown into prison at Pavia, together with his father-in-law, Symmachus, and after six months of confinement, during which he wrote his famous treatise, " De consolatione philosophiæ," both he and Symmachus were beheaded in 525 or 526.* Hawkins and Walther give long lists of his works, the most important of which, as far as we are concerned here, is the treatise " De Musica."

This work, which is evidently unfinished, professes to be a treatise on the music of the Græco-Roman period, but later researches have shown that Boethius misunderstood the subject very largely;† and since the whole of the Middle Ages based their musical studies chiefly upon his treatise, there can be little doubt that it has had a detrimental effect, by delaying the development of the art.

It is founded chiefly on the theory of Claudius Ptolemæus, who lived in the second century A.D., and whose treatise is an explanation of the works of Aristoxenus and Pythagoras; and Ptolemy's work is one of the most valuable we have for the investigation of the Greek scales.‡

Boethius's treatise consists of five " musical books," the contents of which may be briefly summarised as follows:—

Music is intimately connected with human nature, and has an influence on the character and morals for good or evil, according to the use made of it. The state should, therefore, be particularly careful to see that the music used for educational purposes be simple, straightforward, and manly, not feeble, wild, or uncertain.§ The Spartans banished Timotheus, because he

---

* The above dates are from the " Nouvelle Biographie Générale," Paris, 1853, &c.
† Chappell, " Hist. of Music," viii.; Gevaert, " La Musique de l'Antiquité," I., p. 108
‡ Oscar Paul, " Boetius. Einleitung." § Compare Plato's " Republic."

introduced the effeminate chromatic genus, and thus impaired the strengthening effect that music ought to have on the characters of young boys.

Since music cannot be eliminated from our nature, science is necessary in order to direct it in the right way.

There are three kinds of music—that of the spheres (*musica mundana*), vocal music, and instrumental music, such as that of the cythera or tibia. The first kind of music is inaudible to men, and consists of the harmony with which the heavenly bodies perform their allotted courses, by which day and night, the various seasons, and other phenomena are produced.

Vocal music is produced by the harmony and organisation of human voices. The third kind of music is produced by the plucking of strings, blowing of wind instruments, or of those instruments which are set in motion by water (the hydraulic organ), or by striking on a hollow bronze vessel with a rod.

Consonance cannot exist without sound, and sound cannot exist without something striking against something else. Sound is the percussion of the air upon the ear. High or low sounds are produced by the quicker or slower movements of the sound-producing body. Consonance is the reduction to concordant unity, of sounds which are dissimilar in themselves.

The various kinds of proportion, such as sesquialtera, sesquitertia, superbipartiens, &c., are then described in the minutest detail, and those that are fit for harmony are distinguished from those that are not.

Mathematical calculation of sound is more trustworthy than the evidence of the ear; for not every one has an equally correct ear, while even in the same person the correctness of ear occasionally varies.

Chapter x. of the first book contains the story of Pythagoras and the five blacksmiths, whose hammers, being of different weights, produced different notes on the same anvil. So unquestioned was the authority of Boethius all through the Middle Ages, and so averse were students to anything like practical experiments, that Galileo was perhaps the first to point out, that the notes would vary according to the size of the anvil, not that of the hammer, and that, in addition to this, Boethius gives the proportions of the sizes to the intervals wrongly.

The phenomenon of hearing is explained by analogy with the circles of little waves made by a stone, when thrown into a pond of still water. As the stone causes the circles to spread in ever-increasing circumference, but with ever-decreasing wave-magnitude, so is the air agitated by a sound-producing body, and its waves striking the ear cause the sensation of hearing.

There are three species of scale, the diatonic, chromatic, and enharmonic. The diapason or octave is that consonance which has the proportion or ratio of 1 : 2 ; diapente has that of 2 : 3 ; diatessaron, 3 : 4, &c. Here follows a long list of similar ratios and numbers.

In the time of Orpheus, there were four strings on the lyre, the first and fourth of which were tuned in the diapason or octave. The two middle strings were tuned in the diapente and diatessaron.* Others were added, until the number was raised to seven by Terpander, to agree with the number of the planets. Here follow the names of the strings, *hypate, parhypate, lichanos,* &c.

The diatonic species of scale is more natural than the others ; the chromatic is weaker, while the enharmonic is beautiful and tasteful. The chromatic is formed by lowering the lichanos or third string of each tetrachord by a semitone, thus producing a tetrachord consisting of semitone, semitone, minor third. The enharmonic is formed by lowering the two middle notes of each tetrachord in such a way as to produce a succession of quarter-tone (or diesis), quarter-tone, major third.†

Explanations and definitions of various technical terms are then gone into fully, and the construction and signification of consonances. The first book closes with a discussion of the question " What is a musician? " Boethius's opinion will hardly coincide with modern views. He says that the art and theory of music naturally take a more honourable place than its performance. For it is considerably more important and dignified to know the reasons for what a practical musician does, than to do it

---

* At the Paris Exhibition of 1889 the writer heard a band of instruments made of bamboos, and performed on by natives of some Pacific islands, having this scale.

† Later researches have, however, shown that there were several other ways of forming the enharmonic and chromatic tetrachords. See Gevaert, "La Musique de l'Antiquité," Vol. I. ; Westphal, "Aristoxenus " Chappell's " History of Music," &c.

oneself. The mere performer of a work of art, is like a slave, whose master is Science; and if the hand does not do all that Science requires, everything is in vain. A musician, then, is one who does not perform, but who has a sound knowledge of the theory and science of music, and who therefore is in a position of master, and not of the servant who merely carries out manual work. A performer is not named "musician," but "Citharœdus," or "Tibicen," according to the instrument he plays. Even a composer does not rank as a musician: for he makes his songs more by natural instinct than by science.

The second book deals entirely with figures and the mathematical ratios of various intervals; arithmetical, geometrical, and harmonical progressions are treated, together with a mass of matter which concerns the mathematician far more than the musician.

The third book consists principally of a discussion of the nature of the semitone, and an endeavour to prove that Aristoxenus was wrong, who wished to divide the whole tone into two halves by ear; for super-particular proportion (8 : 9) cannot be divided into two equal portions. Again, Aristoxenus is declared to be wrong in saying that the diatessaron consists of two whole tones and a semitone, and the octave of six whole tones.

Philolaus, on the other hand, divided the tone into two portions, in the ratio of 13 : 14.

The remainder of the book, from Chapter vi. to xvi., is given over to a discussion of the semitone, the comma, and the apotome.*

The fourth book shows that sound is produced by motion, and that its pitch is high or low according to the rapidity or slowness of the motion which produces it. In this book also are discussed the proportions of octaves and fifths. The Greek names of notes and the signs used for them are given; the division of the monochord for each of the three species of scale and for each tetrachord. The various species of consonance are again treated in this book, and the Greek modes and transpositions.

The fifth and last book treats of the peculiarities of consonances,

---

* Comma and apotome: portions of a tone respectively smaller and larger than a semitone.

their proportions and the melodic intervals, according to Pythagoras, Aristoxenus, and Ptolemy. From the above summary it will be seen that the study of Boethius could scarcely be of any practical value to the composer or performer. His work is merely an abstruse mathematical speculation, mixed with Platonic ideas of the music of the spheres, and the right place of music in the state, &c. A good deal of it is almost impossible to understand, and it is evident that Boethius himself did not rightly comprehend the Greek authors he borrows from. At the time when he lived Greek music had fallen from its high estate, and Boethius, having no practical acquaintance with it in its best form, could only write from hearsay.

Our Universities were not the only places where the study of Boethius was cultivated. His works formed the basis of nearly all mediæval "speculations" on music on the Continent, as well as in England. The theorist kept apart from the composer, and, in his study, laboured at proportions and mathematical formulæ in the name of music, oblivious of the art which was growing up round him. Our Universities eventually saw that something more was required of a musician than mere mathematics, and by instituting the " exercise " they threw open the Baccalauriat to a large number of those who were more concerned with musical art than with the mathematical proportions of the scale.

CHAPTER IV.

THE MUSIC ACT, MUSIC SPEECH OR LECTURE, AND MUSIC SCHOOL.

As far as can be gathered from early graces, no composition or exercise was demanded from candidates for musical degrees until early in the sixteenth century, at which period the Universities began to grant the degrees only on condition of the performance by the candidate of a specified piece of music in the University Church at "Act time." Apparently this condition was at first imposed, not as a test of the candidate's fitness for a degree, but in order that music might form a dignified and solemn adjunct to the exercises and ceremonies of the Comitia, or Act, and other important public occasions. All the Cambridge graces concerning degrees in music from about 1516 require the candidate to compose a mass, song, or canticum, &c., to be performed before the University in St. Mary's Church, on the day of the Comitia;* and from Wood's accounts† the same conditions prevailed at Oxford.

It was enacted at Cambridge in 1608 that the Comitia or great commencement should be closed with a music Act, "with a hymn by the inceptor in this faculty."‡ And the Oxford statutes of 1636 contain the following enactment: "Concerning the Music Act. After the exercise of the artists (*i.e.*, those who are taking degrees in Arts) in the Act is finished, if there is any who is to take a degree in music he shall perform one or more cantilenas of six or eight parts, with harmony of voices and instruments. This being finished, he shall receive from the Savilian professors the solemnities of his creation."§ The form of supplication mentions that the candidate has "given a concert in five, six, or

---

* *See* App., I, J, K, M, N, O, Q.
† In the Fasti and elsewhere.
‡ Wall-Gunning, "Cambridge Ceremonies," 1828, p. 124.
§ Laud's Statutes, I. Tit., VII., Sec. i., 14.

eight parts in the Music School." Nothing is said as to his having given satisfaction or the reverse. It seems taken for granted that his composition would be worthy of the occasion ; and in some cases we read, notably in that of Chr. Gibbons, that the reputation of the candidate was much increased by his exercise.*

But the Music Act existed independently of the exercise of a candidate for a degree ; and we have several accounts of its being kept by the ordinary members of the University. There is a description of one of these Acts in the diary of Sir Symonds D'Ewes, a fellow commoner of St. John's College, Cambridge, in the early part of the seventeenth century. At the Music Act in 1620 he tells us : " A sophister ' came up ' in the schools, bringing with him a viol, and he commenced his proceedings by playing upon this viol an original ' lesson ' or exercise. After this he entered upon his position of ' sol, fa, mi, la,' which he defended against three opponents. When the opponents had left him master of the field, he played another piece, probably in a triumphant strain, which gave the Moderator occasion to observe that *ubi desinit philosophus, ibi incipit musicus.*" This Symonds has recorded as " a very pretty jest."†

A Music Act was not always forthcoming at Cambridge, but, when there was to be one, it was looked forward to with evident pleasure.

In the Baker MSS., under the year 1658, is a note at the end of the list of graduates, " Dr. Ingelo keeps the act ye next commencement, we shall also have a Music Act."

Anthony Wood gives an account of an Act in which he took part at Oxford on May 14, 1660.‡ " There was a most excellent Music Lecture of the practick part in the public school of that faculty, where A. W. performed a part on the violin. There were also voices, and by the direction of Ed. Lowe, organist of Christ Church, who was then deputy-professor for Dr. Wilson, all things were carried on very well, and gave great content to the most numerous auditory. This meeting was to congratulate

---

* " Christopher Gibbons . . . was then licensed to proceed Doct. of Music, which degree was compleated in an Act celebrated in St. Mary's Church with very great honour to himself and his faculty."—Fasti, 1664.

† D'Ewes, " College Life in the time of James I," p. 104.

‡ Life of Anthony Wood. Ed. by Hearne. Vol. II., p. 529.

His Majesty on his safe arrival to his kingdomes. The school was exceedingly full, and the gallery at the end was full of the female sex. After it was concluded, Mr. Lowe and some of the performers retired to the Crown tavern, where they drank a health to the King, and others. Of the number of performers that were present were Sylvanus Taylor, &c., besides some masters of music."

In 1670 the music at the Act was interrupted by men and women crowding into the railed space in the theatre reserved for the performers,* and an order was given that no one was to pass within the rails unless required by the Professor of Music.

A most important Music Act was held at Oxford in July, 1733, when Handel conducted his "Esther," "Deborah," "Acis," Utrecht Te Deum and Jubilate, part of the Coronation Anthem, and "Athaliah," which last was specially written for the occasion. He was invited to Oxford for this purpose by Dr. Holmes, the Vice-Chancellor, and the fact of the music for the Act being supplied by a stranger roused the anger of Hearne, who says: "One Handel, a foreigner," was allowed the use of the theatre by the Vice-Chancellor " who is much to be blamed, however much he is to be commended for reviving our Acts, which ought to be annual. The performance begins a little after 5 o'clock in the evening: tickets, 5s. This is an innovation: the players might as well be allowed to come and act. Two days later, half-an-hour after 5 o'clock, was another performance in the theatre by Mr. Handel for his own benefit. N.B.—His book (not worth 1d.) he sells for 1s. He performed again on Act Monday, Tuesday, and Wednesday, July 11—13, Mr. Walter Powel, the superior beadle of Divinity, singing with them all alone."†

When Music Acts fell into desuetude, the performance of musical exercises became no longer necessary, although it was kept up till lately as a matter of form. Cambridge finally abolished the performance of Doctors' exercises in 1878, and Oxford in 1890; that of the Bachelor having been previously abolished by both Universities. The performances had long

---

* Wood's Life and Times. Ed. by A. Clark. Vol. I., 73.
† Wordsworth, " Social Life," pp. 200, 201. The University had offered to confer the degree of Doctor of Music on Handel on this occasion, but it was refused by him. The story of his uncomplimentary reason for refusing is shown by Chrysander to be unauthentic.—*See* Dict. Nat. Biog., Vol. XXIV., p. 284.

ceased to have any connection with the public ceremonies, and at Cambridge they were held in College Chapels instead of in the University Church, or the Senate House, as formerly. In Professor Walmisley's time they generally took place in Trinity Chapel, and later in various other chapels; in 1878, for instance, Doctors' exercises were performed in the Chapels of St. John's, Queen's, and King's Colleges.

The Music Lecture, or Speech, was no doubt a survival of the mediæval studies of the quadrivium, on each portion of which the newly created Master or Inceptor of Arts was expected to lecture, and students were required to attend his lectures on music as well as those on the other "arts." Great difficulty was, however, experienced in enforcing attendance at music lectures, and constant dispensations were given for reasons of business, absence from Oxford, press of other work, &c.; and the condition was probably the same at Cambridge. When the *art* of music began to be more cultivated, its *science*, as taught in the Universities, fell into disrepute, and students found it merely a waste of time to study it for the arts degree. The lectures were frequently omitted because there were no listeners;* or they were changed for lectures in another subject, as being more useful.† The unsatisfactory state of the music lecture may be traced back to as early as 1453, in which year the lecturer was allowed to read rhetoric in place of music.‡ There was no connection between the music lecture and musical degrees. Candidates for the latter had then, as now, to obtain their training outside the University, and only visited it for the purpose of performing their exercises and having the degree conferred upon them. But about 1616 the Oxford registrar endeavoured to make a *pseudo*-connection, in order to collect fees from scholars in music for dispensations from these lectures, and apparently obtained a few extra fines by this means.

In course of time, the music lecture came to be given once a year, during Act time, and was often followed by a music act, as we have seen on the occasion when Anthony Wood performed. The lecturer or speaker was chosen annually from among the persons proceeding to the M.A. degree, and was called the

---

* Jan. 20, 1569-70. John Wickham, "Auditores non habet."
† App., S. ‡ Boase, " Reg. Univ. Ox.," 20.

" Prælector publicus in musica." Thus Baker (XXXVIII., 91) records that Matthew Gwyn, the Cambridge " prælector publicus in musica" for 1582, makes a speech in praise of music on October 15 of that year; and Wood gives a list of the Oxford music lecturers from 1661 to 1681, all of whom were persons proceeding to the M.A. degree. Heather's endowment for a lecturer in music was, after the first year of its establishment, given to the person chosen to make the music speech at the Act; and it seems as if Heather himself had some idea of a connection between his lecturer and the ancient custom, for he chose, not a musician, but a Master of Arts, as his first lecturer.

We get some account in Wood of the music lectures of his time. For example, in June, 1679, a dispensation was passed for the music speech and music lecturer to be translated from the music school to the theatre; " and on the 12 July following it was solemnly and well done at 8 in the morning."

July 7, 1680. The music school not being capacious enough, the music lecture was translated to the theatre.

July 10, 1680. " Music lecture and music speech in the theatre; 2,000 people at least; all well done and gave good content. But 'tis a shame that the world should be thus guided by folly, to follow an English speech and neglect divinity, philosophy, &c. Ancient and sober learning decays, as it appears by the neglect of solid lectures to hear an English one in the theatre, and music." *

Wood next gives us a peep at the little jealousies that existed in Oxford. " In July, 1681, Thomas Sawyer, an inceptor of Magdalen, spake the music speech in the music school, whereas for two years before it was in the theatre. The reason as was pretended why he did not speak it in the theatre was because, as the Bishop said, people broke down many things, to the charge of the University; but we all imagined the true reason to be because he was not a Ch. Ch. man, and therefore would not allow him the theatre to grace him. Grand partiality!"

Several of the Cambridge music speeches of last century are preserved. One spoken by the Rev. Lawrence Eusden at a public commencement appeared in a second edition in 1714, with nothing to show when it was actually spoken. Eusden became

---

* " Wood's Life and Times." A. Clark. P. 358, &c.

M.A. of Trinity in 1712, and Poet Laureate in 1718. His speech is in English verse. A famous music speech by Roger Long, M.A., of Pembroke, spoken at the commencement on July 6, 1714, consists of a Latin speech chiefly in praise of Queen Anne, followed by some English verse, "The humble petition of the ladies, who are all ready to be eaten up with the spleen" because they were no longer allowed to sit in the gallery of Great St. Mary's Church; and another set of verses in English, addressed to the ladies, and suddenly breaking off because the "Sons of Harmony" are preparing a feast—*i.e.*, the Concert is going to begin. As no one appears to have taken a musical degree this year, we may presume that this Concert or Music Act was given by members of the University, under the direction of the Professor.

Another speech preserved is that of John Taylor, M.A., of St. John's College, spoken at the opening of the Senate House on July 6, 1730. It consists, like the last, of a Latin speech followed by some English verses addressed to the ladies, and likewise ending with an allusion to the Concert about to commence. This Concert was Dr. Greene's exercise, a setting of Pope's "Ode to St. Cecilia's Day," which was performed in the Senate House at its opening, and the occasion was one of great solemnity.*

The Bodleian Library at Oxford occupies the upper portion of the buildings forming the "Schools Quadrangle." Beneath it are the schools of the seven liberal arts and three philosophies, each school having its name painted in gold on blue ground over the door. Among these is the "Music School," now occupied by the musical portion of the Bodleian Library.

The Music School never had any connection with the teaching of candidates for musical degrees, as its name would seem to imply. It was merely one among the schools of the seven liberal arts. Dr. Heather supplied it with music and instruments (a catalogue of which has lately been found and has been carefully framed and preserved by the present Librarian of the Bodleian), and it was afterwards used for the performance of degree exercises. It was enlarged and modernised in 1780 by Wyatt, under the direction of Philip Hayes, the professor of

---

* Cooper's "Annals of Cambridge," IV., p. 208.

music, who gave three Concerts, one of which consisted of his Oratorio " Prophecy," in order to raise the necessary funds.* About forty years ago the valuable collection of instruments was sold and dispersed, the music removed to the Radcliffe Library, and the room itself was used for examinations. It has now been fitted up for the reception of its collection of music, which forms the nucleus of the musical portion of the Bodleian Library, and the whole is in process of being catalogued.†

* Bloxam, " Reg. Magd. Coll.," Vol. II., p. 222.
† Information from Mr. E. W. B. Nicholson, the Librarian of the Bodleian.

CHAPTER V.

THE ESTABLISHMENT OF PROFESSORS OF MUSIC AT THE UNIVERSITIES.

ONE of the objects of residence at the Universities is that students may attend lectures, and receive tuition in the subjects in which they are to be examined; and Professorships and Lectureships in the arts and faculties have from time to time been established for this purpose. But music has always occupied a position in the Universities peculiar to itself. It has never really ranked as a faculty, and no residence has, as far as can be discovered, ever been demanded for musical degrees; for the residence occasionally required in early graces was quite exceptional, and was not of the nature of that imposed on the ordinary members of the University. The "Scholar in Music" has invariably sought his tuition elsewhere, generally at a Cathedral, or Collegiate Church or Chapel, and has never been under any obligation to attend lectures; his whole connection with the University having been limited to supplicating, performing his exercise, and receiving his degree. Hence, up to 1626, no provision was made for public lecturing on, or teaching of music; for the "Music Lecture" described in Chapter iv. cannot be considered as being intended to instruct candidates for degrees in music. The lectureships in the seven liberal arts (which included music), said by Wood to have been founded by Humphrey the "Good," Duke of Gloucester, in 1439,* seem to have been little more than the ordinary lectures given by the Regent Masters, for which Duke Humphrey supplied 129 volumes.† Hüber says‡ that these were the first chairs established at Oxford, and that they very soon vanished. There is nothing to show what became of them, and it seems open to doubt whether they ever had any special endowments.

---

* Wood, "Hist. and Antiq.," Bk. II., p. 823. Ed. Gutch.
† *See* Appendix, T. ‡ "Die Eng. Universitäten," p. 343.

The first regular Lectureship in Music was founded at Oxford by Dr. Heather in 1626. He was instigated to do this by his friend Camden, who had already (in 1622) founded and endowed the Lectureship in History. The statutes of Laud enact that Dr. Heather's Lecturer in Music shall, once or oftener in a term, lecture on the theory of his art in the Music School, between 8 and 9 a.m.; and on the Vesperies* of the act every year shall hold a solemn lecture in English between 9 and 10 a.m., with intervals of instrumental music. The election of the Lecturer lay in the hands of the Proctors or Vice-Chancellor and was annual. Dr. Heather left £3 per annum as the stipend of the Lecturer, to which was added by Laud's statutes 45 shillings, the sum formerly paid to the Lecturer in Moral Philosophy; and in 1731 £30 per annum was added to this modest salary under the will of Lord Crewe, Bishop of Durham. The first and last Lecturer in the Theory of Music was John Allibond, M.A., of Magdalen College, who read for about a year. After this no one could be found to undertake it, and the stipend was given to the person who made the music speech at the act, and who was elected annually by the Proctors and Vice-Chancellor.†

In addition to the lectureship, Dr. Heather also provided for weekly practices of music under a Choragus, or Prefect of the choir, to take place every Thursday during term, except in Lent, between 1 and 3 o'clock. The Choragus, besides presiding at the practices, was charged with the care of the harpsicon, chest of viols, and music books given by Dr. Heather, and was to bring with him two singing boys every week, and to receive in the music school any who chose to attend for the practice of music. But if no one came the Choragus or "Music-Master" was to rehearse pieces for three voices with the two boys. His stipend was to be £13 6s. 8d. per annum, out of which he was to provide strings for the instruments. The appointment was vested in the Vice-Chancellor, the President of Magdalen, the Warden of New, and the President of St. John's; and these "excellent persons" were to see that the practices were properly carried out; but the first Choragus was chosen by Dr. Heather.

---

* The Vesperies were the last act before taking the degree of Doctor or Master, in which the person about to take his degree disputed with other Doctors or Masters.
† Wood, "Annals," Vol. II., p. 358.

The musical practices soon dropped, and the office of Choragus seems to have involved no duties. The Heather Lecturer had, however, the duty of proposing the grace for candidates to be admitted to take their degrees; but they were presented by the Savilian Professors. That lectures in music were hardly expected is evident; for pains and penalties were imposed by Laud's statutes on all other lecturers for omitting to read, and on students for omitting to attend their lectures, while nothing of the kind was imposed with regard to the Lecturer in Music, who probably soon had no audience.

The following is a list of the Choraguses, who were afterwards called Professors of Music:—

1 Richard Nicholson, Mus. Bac., Organist of Magdalen, elected by the Founder, 1626.

2. Arthur Philipps, Organist of Magdalen, elected 1639, resigned 1656.

3. John Wilson, Mus. Doc., elected 1656, resigned 1661.

4. Edward Lowe, Organist of Christ Church, 1661-1682.

5. Richard Goodson, Mus. Bac., Organist of New College, and afterwards of Christ Church 1682-1718.

6. Richard Goodson, Mus. Bac., son of the last, Organist of Christ Church, 1718-1741.

7. William Hayes, Mus. Bac., Organist of Magdalen, afterwards Mus. Doc., 1741-1777.

8. Philip Hayes, Mus. Bac., afterwards Mus. Doc., Organist of Magdalen, son of the last, 1717-1797.

9. William Crotch, Mus. Doc., Organist of St. Mary's, and sometime of Christ Church, 1797-1847.

In 1848 the offices of Choragus and Professor were separated.

10. *Professor.* Sir Henry Rowley Bishop, 1848-1853.

   1. *Choragus.* Stephen Elvey, Mus. Doc., 1848-1860.

11. *Professor.* Sir F. A. G. Ouseley, Bart., Mus. Doc., 1854-1889.

   2. *Choragus.* Charles William Corfe, Mus. Doc., 1860-1883.

12. *Professor.* Sir John Stainer, Mus. Doc., 1889.

   3. *Choragus.* C. Hubert H. Parry, Mus. Doc., 1883.

In 1856 a third office was created, of Coryphæus or Precentor, probably to take the place of the two boys to be provided under Dr. Heather's statute. This has been held by—

1. Charles William Corfe, Mus. Doc., 1856-1863.
2. Leighton G. Hayne, Mus. Doc., 1863-1883.

The office of Coryphæus was vacant from 1883 to 1891, in which year it was conferred on—
3. The Rev. John H. Mee, Mus. Doc.

By the new statute of 1856, the duties and character of these three musical offices are defined as follows :—

The Professor is to be nominated by the Vice-Chancellor, the Warden of New College, the President of Magdalen, the Dean of Christ Church, the President of St. John's, the Proctors, the Savilian Professors, and the Professor of Poetry, or the greater part of them, subject to the approval of Convocation.

Once, or oftener in each term, he is to read, in the Music School or elsewhere, a lecture on the Theory of Music, with leave to illustrate it by vocal or instrumental accompaniment. He is to receive £100 a year, independently of the Crewe foundation money.

The Choragus is to be nominated by the Vice-Chancellor, the two Proctors, the Professor of Music, and the Public Orator, subject to the approval of Convocation.

He is to hold twice a week in full term, in the Music School or elsewhere, practice for musical students. He is to receive the sum awarded by Dr. Heather, and a portion of the fees paid by the students.

The Coryphæus, or Precentor, shall assist the Choragus. He is to be nominated by the Professor of Music and approved by Convocation. He receives a portion of the fees paid by students.

Dr. Crotch seems to have been the first Professor to give regular lectures, the substance of which, together with that of others delivered in London, he published in 1831. Lectures were regularly given by the late Sir F. A. G. Ouseley, and are continued by the present Professor, with the assistance of a staff of musical graduates ; and these, together with the high standard of examinations for degrees which has arisen during the last twenty years, have raised the post of Professor of Music from little more than a mere name, to a position of importance to the art of music.

The Cambridge Professorship originated in quite a different manner. In 1682 Nicholas Staggins, a musician of mediocre abilities, was granted the degree of Doctor in Music by letters patent of Charles II., of whose band he was the master. His exercise was omitted, through the influence of Dr. James, the Vice-Chancellor, who probably wished to gain favour at Court; but this giving rise to great dissatisfaction and complaints, Dr. Staggins in 1684 composed and performed an exercise. Thereupon the following announcement appeared in the *London Gazette*, No. 1,945: " Cambridge, July 6. — Dr. Nicholas Staggins, who was some time since admitted to the degree of Dr. of Music, being desirous to perform his exercise upon the first public opportunity for the said degree, has quitted himself so much to the satisfaction of the whole University this Commencement, that by a solemn vote they have constituted and appointed him to be a public professor of music there."*

No endowment was made, and no lectures were demanded; and it is possible that in appointing Dr. Staggins " Professor of Music " the University did not intend that the office should be continued after his death. However this may have been, it has lasted to the present day, and, like the Oxford Professorship, has of late years been held by musicians of the highest eminence.

The following is a list of the Cambridge Professors:—

1. Dr. Nicholas Staggins, Mus. Doc., 1684-1705.
2. Thomas Tudway, Mus. Bac., 1705-1730.
3. Maurice Greene, Mus. Doc., 1730-1755.
4. John Randall, Mus. Doc., 1755-1799.
5. Charles Hague, Mus. B., 1799-1821.
6. John Clarke-Whitfeld, Mus. Doc., 1821-1836.
7. Thomas Attwood Walmisley, Mus. Bac., 1836-1856.
8. William Sterndale Bennett, 1856-1875.
9. George Alexander Macfarren, 1875-1887.
10. Charles Villiers Stanford, M.A., 1887.

Wall says † that the election of the Professor is by grace, which passes in two congregations. The grace, describing the candidate's fitness for the post, concludes: " *Placeat vobis ut titulo*

---

* This account is given in Hawkins (p. 739), but the dates are wrong. *See* Appendix, R.
† A. Wall, " Cambridge Ceremonies." Ed. by Gunning, 1828.

professoris in scientia* musica ornetur." Charles Hague was, however, elected by open poll, in 1799, and this method has been generally adopted since. At first the professor's duty seems to have been merely to present candidates for degrees. In 1798, however, we find that he was also expected to examine their exercises. No personal examination took place until 1857, when Sterndale Bennett began to examine candidates for degrees as to their knowledge of music,† as well as their exercises; and in 1868 a salary was for the first time assigned to the Professor of Music. The system thus commenced by Bennett was developed after his death, and further measures were taken with a view to the better cultivation of music as one of the faculties. In 1875 the Council of the Senate, having had under their consideration the regulations regarding the professorship, increased the stipend from £100 to £200, and required the future professor to deliver not less than four lectures annually.

Professor Macfarren gave his inaugural lecture in the Senate House, on May 25, 1875, and in the Lent term of the following year his first course of lectures, the subject being "Form or design in Musical Composition": and similar courses of lectures have been given every year since. The present Professor arranges Concerts at the Guildhall, and Lectures on the Compositions performed there, thus giving a more practical character to the professorial teaching than has been done by any of his predecessors. But besides the Professor's lectures, the Board of Musical Studies has, during the last ten years, arranged courses of lectures on Music and Accoustics, which have been given by Dr. Garrett and Mr. Sedley Taylor: and music, at any rate as far as the theory is concerned, has begun to take an important place amongst the studies of the University of Cambridge. Great efforts are being made to place it on a level in every respect with the other faculties; and no doubt the raising of the standard of requirements all round has had a very beneficial effect on English Music and Musicians.

---

* The word "faculty" is avoided (*see* Chap. v., p. 36), although it is used in the grace creating the professorship.

† The first definite notice of an examination apart from that of the exercise occurs in the following extract from the "University Calendar" for 1857, p. 46: "Proceedings in Music.—The present Professor will hold one examination in each Term, of which due notice will be given to all those candidates who previously send in their names and exercises."

CHAPTER VI.

DEVELOPMENT OF THE MODERN REQUIREMENTS FOR MUSICAL DEGREES.

I HAVE already in Chapter ii. treated of the earliest requirements of candidates for Degrees in Music. It remains to trace them down to modern times. Before the passing of Laud's statutes, the conditions seem to have been very indefinite: but these statutes enacted that seven years (the time given to apprenticeship in any trade) should be spent by the candidate in study or practice, before he was allowed to supplicate for the Bachelorship, and a further period of five years before he could obtain the Doctorate. Still, however, nothing is said about any examination or disputation: all that was required of the Oxford candidate seems to have been the composition, to be performed in the Music School, of which three days' notice was to be given by a "programme" fixed to the great gates of the schools. We find, however, that although not mentioned in the statutes, disputations occasionally took place as a matter of form.*

During the eighteenth century, all studies were much neglected at Oxford,† and it was not till the beginning of the present century that a fresh start was made by means of new statutes,‡ prescribing the forms of examination, due to the energy of Dr. Eveleigh, Provost of Oriel.§

There seems to have been a general depression of learning at Universities during the seventeenth and eighteenth centuries all over Europe. At Padua, about 1715, the candidates for the degree of Doctor in Law were given a paper on which were written the questions *and the answers*, with an indication that

---

* *See* page 70.
† Brodrick, "Hist. Ox.," p. 191, and Ch. xv. of "University Studies in the 18th cent." Ch. Wordsworth.
‡ Ward, "Ox. Univ. Stat.," II., p. 31, &c.
§ Ward, "Ox. Univ. Stat.," II., p. 65.

they must not be answered in any other way: and it was the same with the other faculties. In France, for two centuries, only one candidate was refused admission on account of his ignorance. Hence artisans, and even thieves and robbers, were decorated with the titles of Bachelor and Master. Previously to this, on a certain day of the year, the Master's degree at Paris was given to horse and cow dealers and others who knew nothing of Aristotle, or even the first elements of grammar. At Oxford no one was present at the disputations except those who were officially bound to be there; and it was considered a breach of etiquette if others came. The disputations lasted scarcely half-an-hour, and since they were bound by statute to last from 1 to 3 o'clock, the president, respondent, and three opponents spent the rest of the time in silence or in reading novels.*

Music naturally suffered neglect along with other studies, and it was the last to be taken in hand under the new examination system. To Sir Frederick Ouseley are due many notable reforms† at Oxford, of which the following is a brief outline:—

In 1862 the examination for degrees was more closely defined than before.‡ The candidates for Mus. Bac. were required to pass an examination held by the Professor of Music, the Choragus, and some other graduate, and to compose a piece of music in four parts with organ and string accompaniment, which was to be performed in public. A Bachelor wishing to proceed to the Doctorate§ had to pass an examination and compose a piece in eight vocal parts with full orchestra.

In 1871 two examinations were demanded for the Mus. Bac., and the exercise was to consist of five parts instead of four. In the following year, a critical knowledge of certain classical scores, to be named by the examiners, was added to the requirements, together with some knowledge of history of music. In 1877 the candidate was required, before presenting himself for either of the musical examinations, to have passed responsions, or some equivalent local examination. The credit of initiating this condition is, however, due to Sir Robert Stewart, who had many

---

* Meiner's "Über die Verf. der Deutsch. Üniv. Göttingen, 1801," p. 327, &c.
† Grove's Dict., Vol. II., p. 618A.
‡ "Oxford Univ. Calendar."
§ A candidate for the Doctorate in Music at Oxford was from 1626, but not before, obliged to have previously taken the Bachelor's degree.

years previously established the preliminary "Arts" and history examination and analysis, &c., at Dublin.* Since 1877 no alterations of importance have been made in the Oxford Examinations, except the abolition of the compulsory performance of exercises.

The Cambridge conditions have differed little from those at Oxford, with the exception that the Doctorate might, down to 1889, be taken without the candidate being already a Bachelor.† We have seen (page 39) that examinations were not instituted till 1857, although Cambridge does not appear at any time to have suffered her studies to fall to so low an ebb as Oxford.‡ In 1868 the candidate was required to bring a certificate from some Master of Arts of Oxford or Cambridge, showing that he was qualified both in manners and learning to be admitted a member of the University of Cambridge; § and in 1878 all candidates were required to have passed the " Previous" or some equivalent local examination. Besides this, two musical examinations were imposed instead of one as formerly, and the candidate was required to play from score. A board of musical studies was formed, whose duties were to regulate the examinations in conjunction with the Professor.

In 1878 members of the University were allowed to take the preliminary music examination as their "special" subject for the ordinary degree of B.A., and the final examination for Mus. Bac. began to be looked upon as an "Honour" examination.‖ The performance of the Doctor's exercise was practically abolished in 1878, when the candidate was given the option of performing it or not. Courses of lectures were given, and efforts were made to supply candidates for musical degrees with instruction, in order to induce them to reside and become regular

---

* Grove's Dict., Vol. III., 33b.
† In the University Calendar for 1869, under "Proceedings in Music," is the following notice : " Though usual, it is not compulsory that a candidate in music should first proceed to the degree of Bachelor in Music. He may at once, having fulfilled all the conditions of the University and having very highly (*magnopere*) satisfied the Professor of Music, be admitted to the degree of Doctor of Music.
‡ Wordsworth, "Schol. Acad.," p. 33.
§ The performance of the Bachelor's exercise was abolished this year, and an effort was made to enlarge the choice of subject for the Doctor's exercise, which till then had been of necessity a sacred composition, owing to its performance taking place in St. Mary's Church.
‖ Report of the Board of Mus. Studies. Ap. 24, 1882.

members of the University. The examinations were also thrown open to women, although they were not allowed to take the degrees.

In 1881 all candidates for musical degrees were required to matriculate, and thus become members of the University. Previously to this they had been " in no sense members of the University."* In 1889 it was enacted that no Bachelor of Music might present himself for examination for the Doctorate, until three years had elapsed from the time of his taking his Bachelor's degree, and this is the first intimation that a person might not proceed at once to the Doctorate, without having previously become a Bachelor.

One result of raising the standard of examinations, combined with the general improvement in musical knowledge and appreciation which has taken place during the last twenty years, is seen in the large increase in the number of persons taking degrees in music at both of our Universities. At one time, to be a Mus. Bac. or Mus. Doc. meant little beyond the title ; now it means that the holder has passed several very severe examinations, and although it can be no guarantee that he is possessed of genius, yet it shows that he is highly skilled in the theory and history of his art, and is at least thoroughly competent to do all that can be demanded of a professional musician. It may be said that, with the exception of the playing from score at Cambridge, the Universities impose no practical test ; but this may well be considered as outside their scope. No one could have studied music sufficiently to pass their examinations without having at least a competent familiarity with the pianoforte and organ ; and the teaching and examination of instrumentalists and vocalists may be left to the various colleges of music, whose special province it is to train young musicians.

On June 8, 1893, graces passed the Senate, making radical alterations in the Cambridge degree system, which will come into force as soon as they are confirmed by the Queen in Council. There are to be two examinations for the degree of Bachelor of Music, and the exercise is to be omitted. The candidate must reside nine terms at Cambridge before receiving the degree, and must pass the Previous, or some equivalent examination. The

---

* "Camb. Univ. Reporter"—Report of Council of Senate, May 5, 1881.

existing procedure in the case of the degree of Mus. Bac. is to be retained for seven years, the new system to run concurrently with the old. A new degree of "Master of Music" is created, for which there is one examination, and an exercise similar to the present exercise for Mus. Bac. This degree can only be taken after two years from the date at which the candidate has completed his Mus. Bac. degree. The degree of Doctor in Music is assimilated to the degrees of D.Sc. and D.Litt. The candidate must be not less than thirty years of age, and must have already graduated in some Faculty in the University. He is to make his application to the Chairman of the Special Board of Music, and to send three important compositions upon which his claim to the degree is based; and the Special Board of Music, in conjunction with the Professor, shall decide, upon the merits of these compositions, whether the degree ought to be granted. There will be no examination. The existing procedure for Mus. Doc. will, however, be retained, concurrently with the new system, for five years.

CHAPTER VII.

THE CULTIVATION OF MUSIC AT THE UNIVERSITIES.

Music has been always more or less cultivated at the Universities by others than those taking degrees (who, as we have seen, generally resided anywhere except at Oxford or Cambridge). Although we have no definite descriptions of musical performances in early times, yet ancient inventories and account books, &c., show that the rooms of the students could not have always been without music; and it is probable that in the palmy days of English music it was cultivated here as much as elsewhere.

In Anstey's "Munimenta Academica" several inventories of the goods of Oxford students are given, among which the following items occur:—

Inventory of the goods of Master J. Cooper.   1438.
   Item, una antiqua cithera.
   Item, una "lute" fracta.
Inventory of Symon Beryngton, Scholar.   1448.
   Item, unum hornpipe.*
Inventory of Sir John Lydberg.†
   Item, a lewt.
Inventory of John Hosear.   1463.
   Item, an harpe.

In 1452 Robert the Harpmaker finds sureties that he will not molest Master J. Van, and that he will not enter the house of John Fytz-John at unseasonable hours. That a harpmaker could find a means of livelihood at Oxford shows that there must have been a demand for instruments.

---

   * The hornpipe was a Welsh instrument, called in that language "pibcorn"— *i.e.*, "hornpipe"—because it consisted of a wooden pipe with a horn at each end. Chaucer, in the "Romaunt of the Rose," mentions "hornpipes of Cornewaile." *See* Hawkins, p. 705.
   † "Sir" was the title of a person in Holy Orders.

Frequent mention is also made of organs in Chapels and in the University Church. In 1489 an organ was set up in St. John's Chapel, at a cost of £28. It survived the Commonwealth, and was not pulled down till 1677.* In 1492 the following entries occur in the books of St. Mary's Church:—
"Paid for mending the bellows of the organs, 11d."
"Received of Mr. Waller towards the organs, xxs."
In 1533, there was apparently a regular organist, for we find:—
"To the organ player, 3s. and 4d."
In 1458 Thomas Bentlee, *alias* Deneley, "organ pleyer" of All Souls', got into trouble, for which he was imprisoned for three hours.† These and similar notices are all the accounts we have of music at Oxford in early times, but they show that its cultivation was not neglected.

The reign of Elizabeth, especially the latter part of it, saw English music rise to a higher point of excellence than it has ever attained since. English composers, spurred on by the triumphs of their Italian contemporaries, vied with each other in the composition of some of the finest Madrigals the world has seen. Nor were they behindhand in instrumental music, for their compositions for the virginals, lute, and viols will bear comparison with those of any of the Continental composers of that period. The wave of musical culture which was sweeping over Europe had reached England, and fine compositions poured forth from the pens of such men as Tallis, Bird, Kirby, Wilbye, Weelkes, Hilton, Bull, White, Sheppard, Morley, and many others. Church music, although it undoubtedly suffered by the suppression of the Mass, was well represented by Anthems and settings of the Morning and Evening Services by all the great musicians of that period, who were for the most part organists of the Chapel Royal or Cathedrals, and on the organ they perhaps excelled all their contemporaries.‡

Music was heard everywhere. In the barbers' shops, instruments were kept ready for the use of customers while waiting

---

* Peshall, "Hist. Ox.," p. 129. Another Oxford organ—namely, that of Magdalen College—also survived the Commonwealth, having been conveyed to Hampton Court by Cromwell, and given back to its original owners after the Restoration.
† Anstey, "Munimenta," p. 674.
‡ Ritter, "Gesch. des Orgelspiels," p. 45.

their turn. Every gentleman was expected to be able to take a part in a madrigal, or instrumental piece, at sight; and Elizabeth herself was no mean performer on the virginals and lute. After a dinner-party the guests spent the evening sitting round a table and singing madrigals. Each Ward in the City of London had its regular musicians, whom James I. incorporated into a company. We may take it for granted that music was cultivated at the Universities at this period as eagerly as elsewhere, and at Oxford, at least, the practice of music was continued all through the interregnum. On the death of Charles I. music was suppressed as far as possible throughout the country—organs were destroyed, choirs dispersed, choir books torn to pieces and burnt. It is to this, in conjunction with the destruction of the libraries of monasteries at the Reformation, that is no doubt due the loss of the compositions of the earliest English composers. The libraries were ransacked for choral books of every kind, which, when found, were promptly destroyed, and many masterpieces of English music must have perished.

Professional musicians were obliged to betake themselves to other employments, unless they were fortunate enough to find asylums in the houses of those who were secretly loyal to the art. The Universities suffered with the rest of the country n having all their music books, organs, and other instruments destroyed. But at Oxford, those who loved music practised it to some extent all through these troubled times, and several of the organists who had been deprived of their places managed to pick up a living by this means. Wood gives lists of the names of those who took part in the music meetings at the house of William Ellis,* formerly organist of St. John's College. The instruments used were the lute, theorbo, organ, virginals, counter-tenor-viol, bass-viol, lyra-viol, division-viol, treble-viol, treble-violin (which was only beginning to come into reputation), and harpsicon. Among the performers were William Ellis, Mus. Bac.; Dr. John Wilson, the Heather Professor, "the best at the lute in all England"; Curtseys, a lutenist, ejected from some choir; Jackson, a bass violist; Edward Low, organist of Christ Church (who does not seem to have taken a degree); Glexney, a bass

---

* Ellis's house was "opposite to that place whereon the theatre was built."—Hearne's "Life of Wood," p. 497.

violist and singer, ejected from a choir; John Packer, one of the University musicians, and others. The weekly meetings contributed very much to the improvement of those who frequented them, and were continued till the Restoration, when they gradually ceased, since the " Masters of Music " were all restored to their several places, and the members of the University had no one to lead them. Besides the above gatherings, there were meetings every Friday night of the " Scholastical Musitians " at the various colleges, to which some of the Masters of Music would commonly retire; but these only continued two or three years.

In 1659 James Quin, M.A., died. He had been turned out of his studentship by the visitors, but, singing before Cromwell, the latter was so delighted that he restored him to his place.*

After the Restoration an association of the principal members of the University of Oxford was formed for the promotion of music,† and by means of subscriptions raised by them the Music School was gradually refurnished; for all the old books and instruments had been lost, broken, or embezzled during the rebellion. The following is a list of the instruments and books thus bought:—

An organ with four stops, by Dallans	£51 10
Compositions by Jenkins, Lawes, Coprario, Brewer, and O. Gibbons	22 0
Two violins, with bows and cases	12 10
Compositions by Baltzar and Christopher Gibbons	5 0
Seven desks to place the music on	0 14
A picture, by Taylor, of Christ and the Woman of Samaria	3 0
Pictures of musicians	10 0

Henry Lawes also gave a rare theorbo.

These instruments were preserved in the Music School until about forty years ago, when they were all sold as useless lumber by Dean Gaisford.

The following notices are from Wood's " Life and Times." Edited by A. Clarke. 1891 :—

---

* It is well known that Cromwell was a great lover of music; and no doubt, through his influence, several organs were saved from destruction.
† Hawkins, p. 699.

"On January 11, 1665, Mr. Banister, of London, and divers of the King's Musicians, gave us a very good meeting at the schooles in music, where he hath played on a little pipe or flageolet in consort; which hath been about seven years in fashion; but contrary to the rule in music thirty years ago, which was grave.*

"1671.—On May 18 we had vocal and instrumental music in our theatre, to the new organ set up there—cost £120; made by Smith, a Dutchman.

"1676.—Nov. 5, St. Mary's Church re-opened, all with pinnacles and organs there set up—cost £1,000."

An organ was placed in the gallery of the Sheldonian Theatre in 1669, and "loud music" was performed at the opening of the theatre, followed by speeches, and excellent vocal and instrumental music, to entertain the ladies and the rest of the company.†

The Puritanical party greatly disliked the revival of Church music at Oxford, and compared the organs to the whining of pigs, the singing to that of a jovial crew in a blind alehouse, and said that the devil had appeared several times in a surplice in the cloisters of Magdalen College. In Alicia D'Anver's "Academia" is the following reference to Christ Church in 1691‡—

> The organs set up with a ding,
> The Whitemen roar, the Whiteboys sing.
> Rum, rum, the organs go and zlid,
> Sometimes they squeak out like a pig,
> Then gobble like a turkey hen,
> And then to rum, tum, tum again.

The services, however, had been kept up at Oxford all through the Commonwealth in a sort of homely fashion, and upon the Restoration endeavours were made to restore the church music as quickly as possible. New organs were set up at Christ Church,§ New, and other Colleges, and Ed. Low published a

---

* See also "Pepys' Diary" (ed. by Lord Braybrooke, 1849), Vol. III., 417, and IV., 328. Pepys describes a double flageolet, evidently the same kind of instrument as that played by Banister. A specimen was exhibited and played on by the Rev. F. W. Galpin, at a lecture given by Professor Bridge, at the London Institution, on Jan. 23, 1893.

† Evelyn, "Diary." Ed. by Bray. 1850, Vol. II., p. 40.

‡ "Wood's Life and Times." A. Clarke. P. 357.

§ During the time that Aldrich was Dean of Christ Church (1689-1710) he made every effort to maintain a high standard of efficiency in the choir of Christ Church. He cultivated music with ardour and success, and regarded it as a duty to advance the study and progress of Church Music. He was the possessor of a famous musical library (which he bequeathed to his college), and the composer of many anthems, services, catches, &c.

book in 1661 entitled " Some short directions for the performance of the Cathedral Service." Since boys could not be found ready trained, cornets* were used to supply the soprano parts.

After the erection of the organ in the theatre it was made use of on all State occasions; for instance, when Ludovicus, Prince of Hanover, came to Oxford in 1681, and was presented to the Vice-Chancellor, " the organ played."

The cultivation of music seems to have declined, however, amongst the students during the early part of the eighteenth century, and a taste for " midnight drinkings " appears to have usurped its place,† though there was a large audience when Handel went there in 1733.‡

In 1748 the Music Room was opened, the cost of which was defrayed by public subscription. The following description of it is given in the " Past and Present state of Oxford," edited by Sir J. Peshall:—

" In Holiwell Street stands an elegant stone edifice, appropriated to music, and therefore called the Music Room. Its dimensions are 65 by 32 by 30 feet high. The north end, being a segment of a circle, is occupied by the performers. The orchestra rises gradually from the front, where the singers stand, partly screened by a balustrade. On the uppermost stage, in the centre, stands an excellent organ, built by the late Mr. John Byfield, the bequest of William Frexman, Esq., of Hamels, in Hertfordshire:

"Above, on a plinth, is raised a panel containing an inscription, supported by trophies of musical instruments, rising pyramidally, and finishing with an Apollo's harp, drawn after an antique form found in Pine's ' Horace.' From the orchestra, on each side of the room, run four rows of seats, rising gradually from the floor. The room is chiefly lighted by two very handsome lustres of cut glass, for which we are indebted to the ladies, who raised a subscription of £66 13s. 6d. for that purpose.

" Here are weekly performances of vocal and instrumental music every Monday evening, and the quarterly choral perform-

---

* The cornet of those days was a wooden instrument covered with leather, with a cup mouthpiece and finger-holes. Being very short, it was difficult to play steadily in tune, and its tone is very harsh to modern ears. It was the treble of the serpent. Examples of it exist in most public and private collections.

† Wordsworth, " Social Life," p. 201.   ‡ Page 29.

ances, which are usually oratorios; and these with very little foreign assistance."

There is a collection of programmes in the Bodleian Library, of which the following is a specimen :—

BENEFIT CONCERT.

MUSIC ROOM, FEBRUARY 26, 1789.

ACT I.

OVERTURE—Occasional Oratorio ... ... *Handel.*
SONG—Mr. MATHEWS.
    " Softly arise " ... ... *Dr. Boyce.*
SYMPHONY ... ... *Norris.**
GLEE, Four voices.
    " In vain you tell " ... ... *Geminiani, harmonized by Dr. Hayes.*
QUARTETTO—Flute, Mr. JACKSON ... ... *Lidl.*
SONG—Mr. NORRIS.
    " Let the bright Seraphim " ... ... *Handel.*
CHORUS.
    " Let their Celestial Concerts " ... ... *Handel.*

Between the Acts, (By particular Desire).
CONCERTO, ORGAN, by Master CROTCH ... ... *Handel.*

ACT II.

OVERTURE—" Saul " ... ... *Handel.*
SONG—Master HOLMES (By particular Desire).
    " From thy waves, stormy Lannow " ... ... *Dr. Hayes.*
DUETT—Messrs. NORRIS and MATHEWS.
    " Haste, my Nanette " ... ... *Travers.*
CONCERTO—Violoncello, Mr. MONRO ... ... *Triklin.*
SONG—Mr. NORRIS.
    " From rosy Bowers " ... ... *Purcel.*
CONCERTO 8 ... ... *Corelli.*
CORONATION ANTHEM.
    " God is our Hope " ... ... *Handel.*

---

* This was the Thomas Norris who proceeded Mus. Bac. in 1765. See page 89.

In 1800 the subscriptions had fallen so low that the Concerts were in danger of being given up, but the difficulty was tided over, and they were continued till at least 1819, though in 1818 there was a deficit of £134 8s. 7d. It is said that the Oxford Concerts at the end of the last and beginning of the present century were perhaps superior to any in England outside London, and that a complete orchestra could be formed out of the musicians resident at that time in Oxford.*

What became of the organ in the music room is not known. All the ornamentation described above has disappeared, and the room now presents a bare and desolate appearance.

In 1847 a Society called the Oxford University Motett and Madrigal Society was formed for the practice of sacred choral music and madrigals. Its musical director was Mr. (afterwards Dr.) E. G. Monk, and one of its Hon. Secretaries was Frederick Helmore. It began its meetings at Merton College, but afterwards removed to the music room in Holywell Street. In 1848 C. W. Corfe, Mus. Bac. (afterwards the Choragus of the University), became the musical director. The music practised consisted of the works of Palestrina, Tallis, Gibbons, Bach, Mendelssohn, and others, and public performances were sometimes given, besides which the Chorus for Degree exercises was occasionally supplied by the members of this Society.

The Oxford Choral Society was founded in 1819, and of late years has given many important works, under the conductorship of Mr. Allchin, Sir Walter Parratt, Dr. C. H. Lloyd, and Dr. Roberts.

The Philharmonic Society was founded by Sir John Stainer in 1865, and has also given many important works, under the conductorship of Dr. James Taylor, Organist of New College, and Dr. Lloyd. Symphony Concerts have been given by the Orchestral Association conducted by Dr. C. H. Lloyd.

In 1890 the two older Societies were amalgamated, under the name of "The Oxford Choral and Philharmonic Society," the conductor being Dr. Roberts. Chamber music has, since 1871, been performed by the Oxford Musical Club, and by the University Musical Union, founded in 1884. Many College Concerts of a high class are also given during the year, and

---

* Information from Rev. J. Mee.

probably music never flourished so much at Oxford as at the present time.

Of the music at Cambridge we have not such full accounts as at Oxford. No doubt it was equally cultivated there, but no Anthony Wood has described it. I have already given an account of a Music Act at Cambridge in 1620 (Chap. iv., p. 28), which shows that some sophisters, at any rate, were proficient on the viol, and probably scholars were expected to be able to take their part in a madrigal at sight; and in College accounts frequent charges occur for instruments and their repairs. For instance, in the Bursar's book of Trinity College, 1595-6: "Imprimis, for a sette of newe vialls, viij^{li}. Item, for viall strings and mending the Colledge Instrumentes, xij^s. Item, for a sackbutt and the Carriage, iiij^{li} xj^s.*

When the choral service was restored at King's, in 1660, a chamber organ was temporarily brought from the rooms of Loosemoore, the organist, and afterwards returned to him,† showing that music must have been practised in private during the Commonwealth.

By the end of the seventeenth century concerts seem to have been regularly established; for in 1699 Humfrey Wanley, visiting Cambridge, says that he went to a very good concert, where he was much taken with some Italian songs, brought from Rome by a Mr. Pate, and that a gentleman sang excellently well.‡

In 1710 there was a regular club established at Christ's, at which music meetings were held every week. Uffenbach, who visited Cambridge in the summer of that year, says "There are no professional musicians there, but simply bachelors, masters, and doctors of music, who perform. It is surprising, as they make such ado about music, and even create professors and doctors of music, still this nation achieves scarcely anything in it. I think, however, that their ingenia are not the least musica, as those of all frivolous men; hence, too, all their compositions are very harsh, and cannot equal either the pretty manner of the French, or the tender manner of the Italians. And so, too, this music, both vocal and instrumental, was very poor. It lasted till 11 p.m.; there was, besides,

---

* Willis and Clark, " The Architectural Hist. of Camb.," Vol. III., p. 358.
† *Ibid.*, Vol. I., p. 519.
‡ Wordsworth, " Social Life," 199.

smoking and drinking of wine, though we did not do much of either. At 11 the reckoning was called for, and each paid two shillings."* Uffenbach, however, allowed that the English excelled on the organ. Spinets† and harpsichords were not uncommon in the rooms of undergraduates, both at Oxford and Cambridge, during the eighteenth century.

In 1750‡ there was a correspondence in the "Student" between "Cantab.," who complained of the time wasted in fiddling, and of the foppery of those who were affected by the "scraping cacoethes," and "Granticola," who rejoins that if music were to be put down, the harpsichord, no inconsiderable part of the furniture, must be expelled from the undergraduates' rooms, and Tireman and Randall would then have only the organs of Trinity and King's College to rely on for their subsistence. Granticola also mentions that frequent concerts took place in the halls, which were attended by ladies, and suggests as an additional reason for the practice of fiddling that the fiddler might possibly, in attracting the eyes of the fair, by the display of a white hand, a ruffle, or a sleeve, fiddle himself into a good fortune.

Dr. R. Smith, Master of Trinity, who was the author of a book on harmonics, published in 1749, was, like J. S. Bach, accustomed to tune his harpsichord according to a system of his own. He was the patron and instructor of Joah Bates, Fellow of King's, the director of the original Handel Festival at Westminster Abbey, and the founder of the Ancient Concerts in Tottenham Street. Smith's book treats chiefly of tuning, with the results of experiments on the organ of Trinity College and other instruments. He suggests the use of some instrument, such as that afterwards invented by Maelzel, for counting the beats in a given space of time.

In 1770 Lord Sandwich caused a Concert to be given in Christ's Hall for the benefit of Ximines, a Spanish musician. Wordsworth § quotes the following lines in connection with it from Webb's MS. Collection in the University Library :—

> Now the masters all mount in a terrible row,
> And tuned is each fiddle and rosined each bow,
> And Giardini, when got in his tantrums and fits,
> Frights the poor dilletanti quite out of their wits.

---

* Wordsworth, "Social Life," 199.   † *Ibid.*, 200.   ‡ *Ibid.*, 202.
§ Wordsworth, "Schol. Ac.," 238.

THE CULTIVATION OF MUSIC AT THE UNIVERSITIES. 55

At the harpsichord now Joah Bates takes his place,
Tho' he casts a sheep's eye at his dear double bass;
To the heartstrings it grieves him to quit it so soon,
For though he mayn't play it, he'll put it in tune.

But when he begins to sprawl over a chorus,
And lays the whole matter so clearly before us,
No hearer so stupid but soon understands,
He's full son of Briareus, and heir to his hands.

Charles Jenner sits trembling close to his right side,
And soon as a hard solo passage he spied,
He swore that alone he could do it all right,
Tho' he makes the same blunder but every night.

While Gascoigne, who plays on the hoarse tenor fiddle,
And for ever is coming in wrong in the middle,
With more wit than music is cracking his jests,
Which he thinks better fun than dry counting of rests.

John Beverly* long had been fiddling the bass,
But his fingers so long, seldom hit the right place,
So the great double-bass to take up he did beg,
Where he measures the stops by the length of his leg.

Giardini for absentees now looks about,
If Desborough's called to a worse crying out,
Or if any loose stragglers the practice would balk,
If Rokeby or Ward take a ride or a walk.

Lord Sandwich meantime, ever active and steady,
Eyes the drums with impatience, and cries, "An't you ready?"
Knows who are the alert, and who always ask pardon,
And who are the men must be fetched from the garden.

When the band is all marshalled from front to the rear,
And Miss Ray and Norris and Busy appear;
When impatience to start shines in ev'ry man's face,
Steals in Dr. Shepherd,† a tuning his bass.

But now hushed is each noise, and on each raptured ear,
Break such sounds as the angels stand list'ning to hear;
Handel rouses, and hearing his own Thunder roar,
Looks downward from Heaven, and calls out *encore*.

Several programmes of concerts given about this time in the hall of Trinity College are preserved in Webb's MSS. Concerts were also given at Pembroke, the Master (Roger Long) "having good taste, and much delighting therein; and in the lodge were several apartments well stocked with musical instruments." ‡

The present University Musical Society, which celebrated its fiftieth jubilee in June, 1893, was founded at Peterhouse in 1843,

---

* A notorious Esquire Bedell.   † Master of Christ's.
‡ E. Carter, " Hist. Univ. Camb." 1753. P. 77.

and gave its earliest concerts at the Red Lion in Petty Cury. At first its programmes contained chiefly instrumental music, mixed with songs of the calibre of John Parry's "Nice Young Man." In the early fifties it turned its attention to oratorios, under Mr. Amps, and performed the "Elijah" in 1853, "Antigone" in 1855, &c. Sterndale Bennett occasionally played and conducted the concerts during his Professorship, and from that time the importance of the works performed, and the efficiency of the Society, have shown a steady increase. As early as 1863 selections from "Tannhäuser" were given, and Schumann's Festival Overture (Op. 123) was performed by the C.U.M.S. for the first time in England. In 1873 the present Professor was appointed Conductor, and, by amalgamating the C.U.M.S. and the Fitzwilliam Musical Society, ladies' voices were obtained. In 1875 the custom was begun of obtaining a professional orchestra from London; and from that time the Society has been enabled to maintain a high standard of efficiency and to produce many important works for the first time in England.

Chamber Music has, since 1876, been represented by a series of weekly concerts during term, the performers at which were originally amateurs, but are now mostly professional. In 1889 the Musical Club, an offshoot of the Oxford Musical Union, was founded by R. B. Terry, an Oxford man. Its performers are almost entirely amateur. In addition to these societies, the Cambridge Colleges, like those of Oxford, have given good concerts of late years. Perhaps one of the most important events in the history of Cambridge music has been the establishment, in 1889, by the present Professor of Music, of four orchestral concerts in each year, the performers being drawn chiefly from the London orchestras; and probably more music can now be heard both at Oxford and Cambridge than has ever before been the case in their history.

CHAPTER VIII.

ACADEMICAL DRESS. — DEGREE CEREMONIES, FEASTS.—AN EARLY EXAMINATION FOR THE B.A. DEGREE.

A FEW words on the use of Academical costume, and its connection with the ordinary dress of the Middle Ages, may not be out of place.*

In the twelfth century the ordinary gown worn by men was like that of the Lord Mayor of London, and it had a hood attached to it.† It came into use after the Norman Conquest. Besides the gown, or cloak, a capa, or cape, was used, consisting of a short hooded cloak, which also came from Normandy; and many out-door garments seem to have been furnished with a hood. In the thirteenth century the hood became a separate article of attire, under the Norman name of *chaperon* and *aumusse*, later *amess*. The latter came to be used as a canonical vestment, though by no means limited to this, for it was worn by women for three centuries, contemporaneously with the chaperon. It went out of fashion in France about 1330, but remained long after that among the lower orders in England.

The chaperon worn by men in the reign of Edward II. was a sort of pointed bag, with an oval opening for the face; the point was sometimes of great length, hanging down behind or wrapped round the head. The tail was called a tippet or liripipes. In the first half of the fourteenth century a great variety of hoods was worn, both by men and women; and it is probable that about

---

* This notice of mediæval costume is compiled from Fosbroke's "Encyclopædia of Antiquities" and Planché's "Encyclopædia of Costume."
  † In Planché, page 217, Vol. I., is a representation of a gown and hood of the times of Henry IV. and Henry V. The resemblance of the gown to that of the modern M.A. is remarkably close, the chief difference being that the ancient gown was more ample than the modern.

this time the dress and hood proper to each degree began to be settled at the Universities.

In the middle of the fifteenth century the chaperon lost its pointed shape and became a cap, fitting the head, and having a stuffed roll round it, from one side of which a broad band hung down nearly to the ground, or was passed round the neck and tucked into the girdle; and in the latter part of the century, when caps and bonnets were worn, the hood was slung by the tippet over the shoulder, to be assumed at pleasure. In the sixteenth century it ceased to be worn, but remained as part of the costume of the Order of the Garter, and of legal and official persons and University graduates. By this time it was worn over the shoulder only, at first in its own shape, and afterwards diminishing and changing in form, until it became no longer recognisable as an article of dress that had once served as a head covering. It is now worn hanging on the back, and has for several centuries served to show the particular degree of a University graduate.

Gloves, which are mentioned in all ancient University statutes, were not worn in England before the end of the tenth or beginning of the eleventh century. They were manufactured in Germany, and five pairs made a considerable portion of the duty paid to Ethelred II. by some German merchants in return for the protection of their trade. They were very rare at this time, and were worn only by the highest personages.

In the time of Henry I. gloves are seen having long streamers from the thumbs, but with no separate fingers. They were not generally used in England before the thirteenth century.

The use of jewelled gloves was not uncommon among the higher clergy and other important persons. King John and Edward I. were both buried in jewelled gloves. They were embroidered in the time of Elizabeth, and a finely embroidered glove is preserved in the Museum at Saffron Walden, said to have belonged to Mary Queen of Scots. Gloves were customary as New Year's gifts in the sixteenth century, and, since they were very expensive, "glove money" was sometimes given by persons of limited means in their place.

In all the early lists of fees for degrees at the Universities gloves are mentioned: every new graduate was obliged to give a pair to the Bedells and other officials. Piers, Vice-Chancellor of

Oxford, says to Camden: "We have given Dr. Heather the Oxford courtesy—a pair of gloves, and a pair for his wife."

In 1363 an Act was passed regulating the costumes and amount to be spent on dress for all classes. For instance, tradesmen and yeomen were not to exceed the price of forty shillings per piece for their apparel, and their wives were not to wear any fur, except that of rabbits, cats, and foxes; and so on through all classes of the community. The Universities have at all times insisted on the wearing of the dress suitable to the degree or position of each of their members, and the statutes lay down with great exactness the kind of dress for each degree; but there seems to have often been great difficulty in enforcing the observance of these statutes.

Steven le Scrope, who was Chancellor of Cambridge in 1414, laid down the following rules: No Bachelor in any faculty shall presume to wear in the schools, or processions, feathers, furs, or silk, or other garments of like value, except the sons of lords, and those who are promoted to any ecclesiastical benefice, the value of which is thirty marks. Nor may the birretta,* pileus,† or tena,‡ or any other ornament for the head be worn, and every Bachelor in any faculty shall swear to observe these rules at the time of his admission.

In 1578 no man, unless he was a Doctor, was to wear any hood lined with silk, under penalty of 6s. 8d., and if he refused to pay this fine he could be punished by the Vice-Chancellor for wilful perjury.§

The statutes of Laud enact that no one shall imitate the luxury of those above their condition, and everyone shall abstain from the absurd and arrogant fashion of appearing in public in long boots. There shall also be moderation in the hair, which must not be worn in curls, nor too long.

Undergraduates, clerks, choristers, &c., whenever they appear

---

* The birretta was the ancient headdress of the Italian priesthood and denoted authority (Pulling, "Hist. of the Coif," p. 14). It was worn by Doctors of the Universities and other persons (Fosbroke, "Enc. of Antiquities," p. 936).

† Pileus is the round cap of Doctors.

‡ Tena are described by Ducange as the tassels which are attached to the mitre of a bishop.

§ In 1489 the audacity of the Oxford scholars had risen to such a height that they actually wore hoods in the manner of Masters. A fine of two shillings was imposed for this offence.

in public, shall wear gowns with loose sleeves and square caps; and all graduates shall wear the gown suitable to their degree and the square cap. Models of dresses are to be kept in a chest appointed for that purpose, and tailors shall be forbidden to depart a nail's breadth from them. Fines are to be imposed, according to the degree of the offender, for the non-wearing of these gowns. Doctors in Music are not mentioned in the list of fines, but they would probably rank with Doctors of Medicine.

In 1666 new rules had to be drawn up at Oxford, which were largely directed against extravagance in buttons; for instance, a gentleman commoner was not to wear more than four dozen buttons, nor were they to exceed five shillings a dozen in price.

The Oxford Statutes of 1769 enact that Doctors in every faculty, Bachelors in Divinity, Medicine, and Civil Law, Masters and Bachelors of Arts, likewise Bachelors of Music, shall wear gowns after a pattern which is to be engraved on brass, and lodged in the chest of the Convocation House.

Constant trouble seems to have been experienced about the wearing of proper gowns. For instance, Wood mentions that in 1648 special means were taken to enforce the wearing of academical dress, it having been much neglected; and again, in 1660, the Vice-Chancellor had to issue an order enjoining conformity in this matter.

There seems, until quite lately, to have been no special dress for graduates in music at Cambridge; and the early graces frequently mention the kind of gown in which a candidate wished to be presented for his degree. The grace allowing Wydew to incorporate in 1502 gives him leave to wear a gown of any colour he likes, as long as it is suitable to his degree.*

Christopher Tye was allowed by grace to be presented in the robe of a Non-regent Master,† and to use that of a Doctor in Medicine when appearing in any public assembly.‡ Orlando Gibbons was presented in the gown of a Bachelor of Arts.§ Robert Ramsey was also presented in that of a Bachelor of Arts.|| Dr. Tudway was presented in the gown of a Doctor of Medicine, and Baker remarks¶ that Doctors in Music are usually presented in the dress of a Non-regent Master.

---

* Appendix G.
† Magistri non regentes—those who were not engaged in teaching.
‡ App. M.   § App. O. || App. Q.   ¶ XLI., 219.

Wall, in his account of Cambridge Ceremonies in 1798, says that a Bachelor in Music, on the occasion of taking his degree, wore a full-sleeved gown and a Bachelor's hood. In presenting candidates, the Professor ought to wear the habit of a Doctor of Law or Physic, but Dr. Randall, the then Professor, presented in a gown which was said to be the proper habit of a Doctor of Music, but Wall gives no description of this gown. Professor Clarke-Whitfeld presented in the gown of a Doctor of Civil Law.* In Loggan's Plates, 1675, and in Ackermann, 1814, the Doctor in Music at both Universities is represented as wearing a round cap, and a gown of damasked cream-white silk, lined with satin of a somewhat dark cherry colour, and a hood of the same materials. The Oxford Bachelor's hood and gown seem in Loggan to be the same as those of a Bachelor of Arts, with the addition of ornamental sleeves, and some ornament at the foot. No representation is given of the costume of the Cambridge Bachelor of Music. Ackermann gives no representation of the Oxford or Cambridge Bachelor of Music, but says that their dress is nearly the same as that of the Bachelor in Law.

In 1887 it was recommended at Cambridge that Doctors in Music, when presenting for the degree of Doctor in Music, should wear the Cope.† Up to that time Doctors in Music had ordinarily worn the black gown of a Doctor of Medicine, and it was recommended that they should still continue to do so, but that a double row of Doctor's lace should be added to the collar. The hood of the Bachelor in Music was recommended to be made of satin of the same colour as that used for lining the hood of the Doctor of Music, and lined in the same way as the hood of the Bachelor of Arts.‡ The dress of the Oxford Doctor in Music is laid down by Laud's Statutes as a gown with long sleeves, and a hood of undulating white damascene, with a round silk hat.

The ancient ceremonies in the conferring of degrees were very elaborate, and included a Music Act, a feast,§ the ringing of a

---

* Wall-Gunning, " Camb. Ceremonies, 1828," p. 124.
† The Cope is a robe without sleeves or armholes, bordered with ermine, and it has an ermine hood (Ackermann).
‡ " Camb. Univ. Reporter," 1887.
§ Payments for certain dinners for the Bedells: Bachelors in Music and Medicine and Civil Law paid 22s. ; Doctors in the same faculties, 42s. 4d. Harl. MSS., 7,037, p. 141.

bell, and presenting of gloves. We find little mention of any special ceremonies with regard to degrees in music, except the performance of the candidate's exercise; but they were probably somewhat similar to those of degrees in other faculties.* The feast seems in early days to have occasionally caused trouble, for we find that various statutes had to be made to prevent those who were not invited from throwing stones at the roof, hammering at the doors, and paying other similar attentions.† The custom of giving feasts and gloves was finally abolished at Oxford about 1648, and at Cambridge in 1647, and payments were made in their place. Baker gives the following quaint account of the "Order of the Questionists": ‡ "The determiners of every house do give four pairs of gloves for the Father, the Proctors, and the Bachelor answering. *It.* When the Bedells have gathered in all the gloves, then the Proctors to give each Bedell a pair for their pains. *It.* The senior Mr. Regent or Nonregent replyeth first, both upon the Father and also upon the Bachelor. *It.* All the Determiners do sit in the new Chapell within the Schools from one o'clock till five upon Munday, Tuesday, Wednesday, and Thursday in the week before Shrove Sunday, abiding the examination of so many Mrs. as will repair for that cause hither. And from three to four all they have a potation of Figgs, Resons, and Almonds, Bunns and Bear, at the charge of the said Determiners, whereat all the Bedells may be present dayly. And upon Thursday they be only examined in song and writing. *Item.* The four first Saturdays of Lent every one of the Determiners must come in his Habit and Hood to St. Mary's Church at nine of ye clock, and there sing the common prayer, and offer every day 1d. to the use of the Church. And the Bedell for giving yt attendance have every day 100 oysters and wine to the same."

The candidate for the degree of Bachelor in Music had, as we have seen, no examination of any importance, and was, therefore, probably spared the expense of providing oysters, buns, wine,

---

* "Evelyn Diary," Vol. II., 41, mentions a cap, a ring, and a kiss as part of the ceremonial in conferring the degree of Doctor in Music. They formed also part of the ceremonies of conferring the Doctorate in any faculty at German Universities. "Ersch and Grueber Encycl., 1835," Vol. I., p. 240.

† Anstey, "Munimenta Academica," p. 308.

‡ Harl. MSS., 7,037, p. 103. Questionists are those about to be examined for the Bachelor's degree.

beer, &c., but he had to pay for gloves, bellringing, and a feast,* and the Doctor in Music had to pay higher fees than the Bachelor for these purposes. The fees for the Master in Grammar included no feast and no gloves, and amounted to less than half those for the Bachelor in Music, and this, together with the arrangements made with regard to dress, seems an additional argument against the degrees in music being comparable to those in grammar.

---

* *See* p. 14, *note.*

CHAPTER IX.

OXFORD GRADUATES IN MUSIC.

IN this and the next chapter I have given a chronological list of all those musicians whose names are recorded as having taken degrees in music at Oxford and Cambridge from the year 1463. The list is probably very imperfect, as, down to the beginning of the present century, the registers rarely recorded musical degrees, and in many cases the only means of finding out dates and other particulars has been to consult the Grace-books, which occasionally contain references to these degrees. At Oxford, degrees in music were systematically omitted from the registers between 1763 and 1800, probably because they conferred no membership of the University upon the holder, and were looked upon as outside the regular course of things. The University Calendar of Cambridge, of the latter part of the last and the beginning of the present century, contains no information as to "Proceedings in Music," and the editor frankly confesses that he can find out nothing definite about them, or the dress to be worn by musical graduates; and down to 1860 the names of the few graduates which occur in the Calendar are exceptions to the general rule, which was to omit them altogether. I have naturally derived great assistance from Foster's "Alumni Oxonienses" and from the Cambridge "Catalogus Graduatorum," which commences with 1659, and for the short biographical notices I am chiefly indebted to Sir George Grove's "Dictionary of Music," the "Dictionary of National Biography," and Brown's "Biographical Dictionary of Musicians."

It will be seen that at both the Universities, about the year 1870, there was a great increase in the number of those who took degrees in music, a fact no doubt partly due to the raising of the standards of examination and the higher value of the degree in consequence; and partly, probably, to the increase in appreciation and better cultivation of music throughout the United

Kingdom. Whatever the cause of this increase may have been, it marks a distinct epoch in the history of the degrees, and possibly of English music as well.

1499 (*circa*).

Mus. Bac.—Robert Wydow, who incorporated at Cambridge in 1502. *See* p. 121.

1502 or 4.*

Mus. Bac.—Henry Parker, Magd. Hall. Wood says he was eminent for his vocal and instrumental compositions, some of which were in the library of the Music School. A *Richard* Parker, probably a relation, was Organist of Magd. Coll. in 1500.

1505.

Mus. Bac.—Thomas Goodman,† called John by Wood. He was noted for his compositions.

1506-7.

Mus. Bac.—Richard Ede, a regular Canon, who had studied for ten years, supplicated that the reading of Boethius might suffice for his admission to the degree. He was, however, required to compose a Mass with Antiphona, to be sung before the University; but it is not known if he was admitted.

1508-9.

Mus. Bac.—John Mason, B.A., a regular Canon, Instructor of the Choristers at Magdalen in 1508; Chaplain in 1509; Canon of Hereford, 1525; Prebendary of Pratum Minus and Putston Minor, 1525. He is mentioned by Morley in his catalogue of famous musicians as " Sir " John Mason, " Sir " being the epithet of a cleric. He died in 1547 or 1548.‡

Thomas Scherman, or Sherman, called John by Wood, a secular Chaplain, supplicated, but it does not appear whether he was admitted.§

---

* In the Fasti, Wood gives this date as 1502, but in his MS. list of graduates (Ashmol, E. 5) he gives it as 1504.

† " Boase Reg.," p. 292, "*eodem die* (June 26) *admissus est in musica Thomas Goodman.*"

‡ Foster, " Alumni," and Bloxam, II., 3, 125, 182. In the library of Peterhouse, Cambridge, there are four compositions by John Mason, a Cistercian.

§ Fasti.

1509.

Mus. Bac.—John Wendon, a scholar in music, whose grace was granted on condition of his composing a Mass, to be sung at the following Act.*

Mus. Bac.—John Clawsey. Both he and Wendon were eminent in their profession.*

1510-11.

Mus. Bac.—John Gilbert, or Gylbart. "His order and place are not set down."*

1511.

Mus. Doc.—Robert Fayrfax, incorporated from Cambridge. *See* page 120. This is the earliest recorded degree of Mus. Doc. granted at Oxford.

Mus. Bac.—John Dawke.

1512.

Mus. Bac.—John Dygon, a Benedictine Monk.* Nine persons of this name appear about this time, one of whom was Prior of St. Augustine's, at Canterbury, and it is impossible to say which was the musician. Hawkins gives a Motet by him, "Ad lapidis positionem," which shows that he was a very skilful composer.†

1513.

Mus. Bac.—Christopher Wodde, or Wood, supplicated, but it is doubtful if he was admitted.*

1515.

Mus. Doc.—Robert Porret, or Perrot, B.A., Organist of Magd. Coll., who was already a Mus. Bac. of Cambridge (*see* page 121), supplicated, and his request was granted on condition of his composing a Mass and one song.* He was of an ancient and knightly family of Haroldston, near Haverfordwest, but was born at Hackness, in Yorkshire. In 1519 he was Instructor Choristarum of Magdalen. In 1534 he was appointed Receiver-General of the Archdeaconry of Buckingham, and at one time he was Principal of Trinity Hall, a religious house at Oxford. Died 1550.‡

---

* Fasti.
† Hawkins, p. 358. *See* also Grove's Dict., Vol. IV., page 625.
‡ Bloxam, "Reg. Magd. Coll.," Vol. II., p. 182.

1516.

Mus. Bac.—Henry Petre, or Peter, a secular Chaplain who had spent thirty years in the study and practice of music. He is perhaps the person referred to in the Cotton MSS. as "a most excellent Notator."*

1516-17.

Mus. Bac.—John Draper supplicated, and his request was granted, with one or two conditions.†

1518-19.

Mus. Bac.—John Charde, who was a student sixteen years and had composed a Mass and Antiphona of five parts, supplicated that this should suffice to allow him to be admitted to the reading of any book of Boethius. He was required to give the Mass and Antiphona into the hands of the Proctors and to compose another Mass in five parts on "Kyrie rex splendens." He is the first Bachelor who composed in so many parts.

1519.

Mus. Bac.—Thomas Pen, a regular Canon.

Thomas Janys, or James.

Whether these two persons had their supplication granted is not known.

1521-22.

Mus. Bac.—John Sylvester, esteemed very eminent in his profession.

1524.

Mus. Bac.—William Chell, a secular Chaplain, Precentor and Prebendary of Hereford Cathedral, writer of two tracts, called *Musicæ practicæ compendium* and *De proportionibus mathematicis*, probably copied from John Dunstable and John Otteby. When Elizabeth came to the throne he was deprived of his Cathedral appointments, and disappears. Copies of the above works are in the British Museum and at Lambeth Palace.‡

1524-5.

Mus. Bac—Henry Young, or Yonge, a student of music, supplicated, but apparently was not admitted.

---

* Hawkins, p. 238. † Fasti. ‡ Dict. Nat. Biog.

1528.
Mus. Bac.—John Whyte.

1531.
Mus. Bac.—James Northbrooke, a secular Chaplain.

Mus. Bac.—Thomas Taylor, a secular Chaplain, supplicated, but it is doubtful if he was admitted.

Mus. Doc.—John Gwyneth, or Gwynneth, or Guinneth, a secular priest, a native of Wales, of very poor parentage. He was aided in his studies by some beneficent clergyman. He supplicated for his degree on the grounds of his having spent twelve years in the study and practice of music, of having composed all the responses for the whole year in Division Song, and of having published many Masses in that Song. His request was granted on condition that he composed one Mass against the Act following; but he supplicated again, that whereas he had spent twenty years (the number seems to have increased with the urgency of the demand) in the practice and theory of music, and had published three Masses in five parts and five Masses in four parts, and divers Symphonies and Antiphonas and Songs for the use of the Church, he might be admitted to proceed. The second supplication was granted on condition that he pay to the University on the day of his admission 20 pence, having done which he was licensed to proceed. Burney says that there are some fragments of two-part counterpoint by a Joseph Guineth in the Pepys Library at Cambridge, in which red notes are used for diminution. In 1533 he was presented to the Rectory of St. Peter, Westchepe, where he wrote some controversial tracts against heretics.* Morley mentions him among eminent musicians. It will be observed that no mention is made of his holding the Bachelor's degree previous to supplicating for the Doctorate, and that he based his claim to the latter on his reputation as a composer.

1535.
Mus. Bac.—Thomas Mendus, or Mend, a secular Chaplain, was admitted to the reading of any musical book of Boethius.

Mus. Bac.—Thomas Brightwyn, a secular Chaplain, supplicated, but it is doubtful if he was admitted.

---

* Fasti, "Ath.," I., 246, ed. Bliss; "Lansdowne MSS.," 980, f. 231; "Ox. Hist. Soc., I., 167.

1548.

Mus. Doc.—Christopher Tye, incorporated from Cambridge. *See* page 122.

The records from 1536 to 1549 are lost, and those of the succeeding years are very imperfect, " having been neglected by one who was afterwards deservedly turned out of his place " (Wood, " Ath.").

1550.

Mus. Doc.—John Marbeck, or Merbecke.* He was famous for his writings against Popery as well as for his music, and while Organist of St. George's Chapel, Windsor, was, about 1544, condemned to the stake, together with Person, a priest, Testwood, a singing man, and Filmer, a tradesman. Marbeck escaped through the influence of Gardiner, Bishop of Winchester, while the other three were executed. He takes an important place in the history of English Church music, as being the first to set the whole of the Cathedral Service to music, which he published in 1550 under the title of " The booke of Common Praier Noted." Burney gives copious quotations from this work (which is an adaptation of the ancient Plainsong to the English service) in his second volume, page 578, &c. Hawkins gives a three-part hymn by Marbeck, " A virgine and Mother," † and there are portions of a five-part Mass by him in Burney's " Musical Extracts " in the British Museum. He died about 1585.

1554.

Mus. Doc.—John Shepeard, or Sheppard, who had been a student of music at Oxford for twenty years, and had composed many *Cantiones*. His grace was granted, but it does not seem that he took the degree, for in the succeeding year he is mentioned in official documents without the title of Doctor.‡ Grove's Dictionary makes him a Mus. Bac., but in his supplication for the degree of Mus. Doc. he is called simply "studiosus musices." He was Organist, Choirmaster, and Fellow of Magdalen College. Morley includes him among famous

---

* Grove's Dict., Vol. IV., p. 717. † P. 451.
‡ Bloxam, " Reg. Magd.," II., pp. 187, 188.

Englishmen. Burney and Hawkins give specimens of his compositions,* of which a considerable number is extant in Day's "Morning and Evening Prayer," 1560; "Whole book of Psalms," 1563; in the Music School at Oxford, in the British Museum, and the Library of the Royal College of Music.

1583.

Mus. Bac.—William Millar, who had been twenty years a student.

1585.

Mus. Bac.—Nathaniel Giles, born about 1550. Chorister, then Clerk of Magd. Coll., afterwards Organist and Master of the Choristers of St. George's, Windsor. In 1597 he succeeded Hunnis as Master of the Children of the Chapel Royal. His supplication for the Doctorate in 1607 was granted on condition of his composing and performing a choral hymn in eight parts at the Act; but he failed to do this for some reason, and did not proceed to the higher degree till 1622. On this occasion the following questions were appointed to be discussed between him and Dr. Heather: "Whether discords were to be allowed in music? 2. Whether any artificial instrument can so fully and truly express music as the natural voice? 3. Whether the practice be the more useful part of music or the theory?" These questions, however, were not actually discussed, being merely a matter of form. Wood remarks† that he was as "noted for his religious life (a rarity in musicians) as for the excellence of his faculty." His compositions consist of some contributions to Leighton's "Teares and Lamentacions of a sorrowfull Soule," 1641, and some MS. Anthems. Hawkins, page 961, quotes his "Lesson of discant on the plainsong of Miserere." Other compositions are in Barnard's Collection, the Fitzwilliam and British Museums,‡ and in other MS. collections. He died January 24, 1633-4. (*See* Grove's Dictionary and "Dictionary of National Biography.")

Mus. Bac.—Mathew Godwin. Twelve years a student.

---

* Burney gives a motet, "Esurientes implevit bonis," Vol. II., 587.
† Fasti, anno 1622. ‡ "Add. MSS." 29,372.

1586.

Mus. Bac.—John Bull, who had practised music fourteen years. "This person, who had a most prodigious hand on the organ, and was famed throughout the religious world for his Church music, was trained under an excellent master, Blitheman, organist to Queen Elizabeth."* After taking his degree at Oxford he proceeded Mus. Doc. at Cambridge, and incorporated at Oxford in 1592; he would have proceeded Doctor in the ordinary course at Oxford "had he not met clowns and rigid puritans, who could not endure Church music."† In 1582 he was appointed Organist of Hereford Cathedral; 1585, member, and 1591, Organist of the Chapel Royal; 1596, first Gresham Professor, which post he was obliged to resign on his marriage in 1607. In 1601 he went abroad and greatly increased his reputation as an organist and composer. At St. Omer's, while travelling incognito, he is said by Wood to have added in a few hours forty parts to a composition already written in forty parts, whereupon the composer "swore by the great God that he that added those parts must either be the Devil or Dr. Bull."‡ In 1611 he appears as a member of the household of Henry, Prince of Wales, brother of Charles I., with a pension of £40. In 1613 he "went abroad without license," became Organist at the Chapel Royal at Brussels, and afterwards succeeded Waelrent at Notre Dame, in Antwerp, in which post he apparently continued till his death in 1628. Many of his compositions, both vocal and instrumental, are extant: in Leighton's "Teares and Lamentacions"; in "Parthenia," in the so-called "Queen Elizabeth's Virginal Book" § in the Fitzwilliam Museum; in Peterhouse Library, at Christ Church, and the Music School at Oxford; in a collection published by Phalêse, at Antwerp, 1629, entitled "Laudes Vespertinæ B.M. Virginis"; in Boyce's Cathedral music; at Buckingham Palace, the Royal College of Music, and in a volume at the British Museum ("Add. MSS.," 23,623), said to have belonged to Queen Caroline, in which the dates

---

* Fasti.   † Ibid.   ‡ See Hawkins, p. 480.
§ For an account of this famous book, and index of the pieces in it, see Grove's Dict., IV., 305.

of the compositions, and, in one case, the organ stops, are given. His supposed authorship of the National Anthem was discussed in the *Musical Times* in 1878. A very complete account of his life is given in the "Dictionary of National Biography," Vol. VII.

Mus. Bac.—Benjamin Hamm was allowed this degree on condition of his composing a Choral Hymn of eight parts before Passover following.

Mus. Bac.—John Munday, of Christ Church, one of the Organists to Queen Elizabeth, and successor to Marbeck, at Windsor, about 1585. He was held in "high esteem," both as a theorist and a practical musician. He published, in 1594, "Songs and Psalms composed into three, four, and five parts, for the use and delight of such as either love or learne musicke." Burney gives a part-song by him, "In deep distresse."* In 1624 he took the degree of Mus. Doc. Compositions by him are contained in the "Triumphs of Oriana," Barnard's MS. Collections, Burney's MSS., and the so-called "Queen Elizabeth's Virginal Book." He died 1630.

1587.

Mus. Bac.—Robert Stephenson, or Stevenson, who was thirty-three years a student, and had supplicated in 1583. He took the degree of Mus. Doc., 1596.

1588.

Mus. Bac.—Thomas Morley, born 1557, a pupil of Bird. In 1592 he became Gentleman of the Chapel Royal; in 1598 he obtained a patent for the exclusive right of printing music books. He was a prolific composer of madrigals, church and instrumental music, much of which has been republished in modern times. He occupies an important position in musical history through his "Plaine and Easie Introduction to Practicall Music," published in 1597, the first regular treatise on music published in England. This work contains many things relating to ancient notation which are not found

---

* Vol. III., p. 55.

in other treatises of his day. Several editions of it have been published, and in the seventeenth century it was translated into German, under the title "*Musica Practica*," by J. C. Trost. Morley died in 1604. Fétis* places him above Bird in merit as a composer, and considers that he had profited much by the study of the works of Palestrina.

Mus. Bac.—John Dowland, of Christ Church. Born about 1562; died, 1625 or 1626. "The rarest musician that his age did behold." He was, probably, the most famous performer of his day on the lute, for which instrument he composed and published a great deal of music. In 1581 he travelled in France and Germany, where he was received in a most flattering manner by the Duke of Brunswick and by Prince Maurice, Landgrave of Hesse. He then went to Italy and made acquaintance at Venice with Giovanni Croce, and at Rome with Luca Marenzio. About 1599 he went to Denmark, where he became first lutenist to the King. In 1605 he returned to London and published his "Lachrymæ" for lute and viols, and, after another visit to Denmark, he finally returned to London in 1609, and remained till his death, the date of which is not known. In the same year he published a translation of Ornithoparcus' "Micrologus." His compositions, which chiefly consist of "Songs or ayres" for voices or instruments, are more of the nature of glees than madrigals; that is, they depend more for their effect on their being harmonised melodies than on their counterpoint. MSS. are to be found in the British Museum, at Christ Church, the Fitzwilliam Museum, and Cambridge University Library.

1592.

Mus. Bac.—Giles Farnaby, of Christ Church, a famous performer on, and composer for, the spinet and virginals. Many of his pieces are in "Queen Elizabeth's Virginal Book." Little is known of his life except that he was of a Cornish family. His compositions are, besides the pieces above-mentioned, some contributions to East's "Whole booke of Psalms,"

---

* "Biog. Universelle des Musiciens."

1592; canzonets, 1598; an anthem in the British Museum ("Add. MSS.," 29,427).

Mus. Bac.—Richard Reade, or Read, a composer of services. He was required to compose a hymn in six parts for the use of the University before taking his degree.

Mus. Bac.—George Waterhouse supplicated, and was probably admitted. He was Organist of Lincoln Cathedral and afterwards of Elizabeth's Chapel. Morley says that he made above a thousand canons on the plainsong of *Miserere*, "which for varietie surpassed all that had gone before." Not a single composition of his is extant, although Morley praises him highly as a composer. He died 1601.

Mus. Bac.—The Rev. Edward Gibbons, incorporated from Cambridge. It is not known when he took this degree there. He was born about 1570, became Organist, Priest-Vicar, Sub-Chanter, and Master of the Children at Bristol Cathedral about 1592. He was Organist of Exeter Cathedral from 1611 till 1644, when the organs were suppressed. An anthem by him is in the Tudway Collection. Matthew Locke was his pupil, and he was an elder brother of Orlando Gibbons.

Mus. Doc.—John Bull, incorporated from Cambridge. *See* p. 71.

1593.

Mus. Bac.—Arthur Cock, or Cocke, Organist of Exeter Cathedral, supplicated February 25, 1593-4, and his grace was granted.

1593-4.

Mus. Bac.—Matthew Jeffrye, or Jefferies, Vicar-Choral of Wells, supplicated, and was required to compose a choral hymn in six parts.

1595.

Mus. Bac.—Francis Pilkington, of Lincoln College, a famous lutenist, and author of the " First book of Songs or Ayres of four parts with Tablature for the Lute or Orpharion, with the Violl da gamba."

1595-6.

Mus. Bac.—Richard Nicholson, of Magdalen College. He afterwards became the first choragus under Dr. Heather's endowment. He was the composer of several madrigals, some of which are in the " Triumphs of Oriana." He died 1639.

1596.

Mus. Doc.—Robert Stevenson, Mus. Bac., was licensed to proceed Doctor. See p. 72.

1597.

Mus. Bac.—Robert Jones, St. Edm. Hall, sixteen years a student,* a celebrated lutenist. He contributed to the "Triumphs of Oriana" in 1601, and in the same year published a collection of "Ayres." In 1607 he published madrigals for viols and voices, and in 1609 and 1611 "Books of Ayres for the Lute." He also contributed to Leighton's "Teares and Lamentacions" in 1614. It is not known when he died. A copy of his "Ultimum Vale," or "3rd book of ayres," is in the Royal College of Music; and there is some music by him in a MS. in the British Museum (App. to Royal MSS., 63).

1599.

Mus. Bac.—Robert Barker, Merton College, sixteen years a student.

1600.

Mus. Bac.—Henry Porter, of Christ Church. He was ejected from his appointment during the Rebellion, and was supported in his old age by Edward Laurence, Esq.† Wood does not mention what his appointment was.

1602.

Mus. Bac.—Thomas Weelkes, of New College, Organist of Wykeham's College, Winchester. Nothing is known of his life or the time of his birth or death. He was one of the most eminent of the madrigal writers, and his compositions, which are numerous, are still very popular, and several have been republished of late. Besides his published collections, he contributed to Leighton's "Teares and Lamentacions," Barnard's Collection, and there are MSS. of his compositions at the Royal College of Music and the British Museum.

1603.

Mus. Bac.—Thomas Boyse, or Boys, of All Souls', a composer of Church services.

---

* Clark, "Reg. Univ. Ox.," II., 147.   † Fasti.

1604.

Mus. Bac.—John Daniel, of Christ Church. Some of his compositions were in the Music School in Wood's time.

1605.

Mus. Bac.—William Wigthorpe, New College, ten years a student.

1607.

Mus. Bac.—Thomas Tomkins, Magd. College, son of the Rev. Thomas Tomkins, Chanter in the choir of Gloucester. Born 1586; died 1638. His family produced more musicians than any other in England. He was a pupil of Bird, successively Chorister, Clerk, and Usher of Magdalen, Gentleman of the Chapel Royal, and afterwards Organist of Worcester Cathedral. Burney describes him as an excellent contrapuntist, who supplied the Church with many admirable compositions. His compositions consist of part-songs, anthems, and hymns. Some of his Church music is in MS. at Magdalen College, Oxford; and a MS. collection of his pieces for organ and virginals was in the possession of a M. Farrenc.* There are also MSS. in the Tudway Collection, at Ely and Christ Church.

1608.

Mus. Bac.—William Stonard, Organist of Christ Church. He was required to compose a choral hymn of eight parts for his degree. Some of his compositions are in the Tudway Collection, in Clifford, and in the Music School at Oxford. The dictionaries of Grove and Brown, following Hawkins, say that he took the *Doctor's* degree in 1608. There is nothing to show that he ever became a Doctor of Music.† He died 1630.

1610.

Mus. Bac.—Thomas Bartlet, or Bartlett, of Magd. College, composer of a " Booke of Ayres with a Triplicitie of Musicke,

---

* Fétis, " Biog. Univ. des Musiciens."
† See Fasti, and Clark, "Register Univ. Ox.," Vol. II., 147. The mistake arose, probably, through the wording of Wood's MS. list of graduates, where Stonard simply occurs as " admissus," immediately after a long account of Nat. Giles' supplication for the Doctorate.

whereof the first part is for the Lute or orpharion and the Viole de gamba, and 4 parts to sing; the second part is for 2 trebles to sing to the Lute and viole; the third part is for the Lute and one voice and the Viole de gamba." Published in 1606.

Mus. Bac.—Richard Deering, or Dering, of Christ Church. He was educated abroad, and his first composition, "*Cantiones sacræ cum basso continuo*," was published at Antwerp in 1597. This was probably the first work printed with figured bass.* Mace says that before the "scoulding violins" were allowed to perform in concerts at Cambridge, Dering's compositions were in great favour. He became Organist to the English nuns at Brussels in 1617, and to Henrietta Maria on her marriage with Charles I. in 1625. He died in 1630. A large amount of his music exists in MS. at Christ Church, the Oxford Music School, the Royal College of Music, Peterhouse, and the British Museum. His published works are a second set of "Cantiones Sacræ," in 1617; "Cantica Sacra," 1618; "Cantiones Sacræ," 1619; "Canzonette," 1620. Cromwell was a great admirer of his works.

1612.

Mus. Bac.—John Allen, Organist of Chester Cathedral. He was required to compose a song in seven parts for his degree, to be sung in St. Mary's Church at the next Comitia.

1613.

Mus. Bac.—Martin Pearson, Pierson, or Person, of Lincoln College, Master of the Choristers at St. Paul's when John Tomkins was Organist. He published, in 1630, "Mottects or Grave Chamber Musicke for voyces and vials, with an organ part, which may be performed on virginals, base-lute, bandora, or Irish harpe." He seems to have become rich, for he left the poor of Marsh, in the Isle of Ely, £100, probably because he was born there. Some of his music is in the "Teares and Lamentacions" of Leighton. He died 1650.

---

* "Dict. Nat. Biog.," Vol. XIV., 398.

Mus. Bac.—John Amner, who was appointed Organist of Ely Cathedral in 1610. He died at Ely 1641. His compositions are preserved at Ely, in the Tudway and other collections in the British Museum, at Peterhouse, and Christ Church. He published, in 1615, a collection of Sacred Hymns for voices and viols. Burney says that he also published some madrigals.*

1616.

Mus. Bac.—John Lake, of New College. He was required to compose a choral hymn of five parts for his degree, but he was not admitted.†

Mus. Bac.—John Vauler, or Vauter, of Lincoln College, who was required to compose a choral hymn of six parts.

1619.

Mus. Bac.—Richard Emot, or Emmot, of Brasenose, supplicated, but it is not known if he was admitted. He had been a student for twenty years, and had some appointment at Wells Cathedral. Wood says he made several compositions for voices and instruments, but none seem to have been preserved.

1622.

Mus. Bac. and Mus. Doc.—William Heather, or Heyther, called Richard in the Register,‡ an intimate friend of William Camden, then Headmaster of Westminster. He was deputed by Camden, in 1622, to carry a deed of gift to Piers, the Vice-Chancellor of Oxford University, founding a Lectureship in History. In return for this the Convocation conferred on Heather, who was a musician by profession, and a Gentleman of the Chapel Royal, the degrees of Bachelor and Doctor of Music. This is the first recorded instance of "accumulation" of the two degrees. It is said that Heather's exercise was written for him by Orlando Gibbons, who took the degree of Doctor of Music at the same time; and Mr. W. H. Cummings is in possession of a copy of Gibbons' Anthem "O clap your hands," with the inscription—" Dr. Heather's commencement song, composed by

---

* Vol. III., p. 326. † Ashm. Mus., E. 5.
‡ A. Clark, " Register Univ. Ox.," Part i., p. 148.

Dr. Orlando Gibbons." The probability is that since Heather's degree was of an honorary nature, and was given at Camden's request as a return for a very munificent gift to the University, Convocation allowed this irregularity; and, in addition, they paid all Heather's expenses and gave him a pair of gloves for himself and his wife.* He was born about 1563, and was a chorister at Westminster. On February 20, 1626, he founded the Lectureship and "Mastership" of Music at Oxford, which afterwards became the present Professorship, of which an account is given in Chapter v. He died in 1627, and was buried in Westminster Abbey. Besides founding the Professorship at Oxford, he left charitable bequests to Eton College, to members of the Chapel Royal, in case they should ever be in need, and to the hospital in Tothill Fields. He does not appear to have been a composer.

Mus. Doc.—Orlando Gibbons, who graduated as Mus. Bac. at Cambridge in 1606. See p. 125.

Mus. Doc.—Nathaniel Giles. See p. 70.

1623.

Mus. Bac.—Hugh Davies, of New Coll., Organist of Hereford Cathedral. Wood says that he was eminent for his Church compositions, but does not mention what they were. He died about 1644.†

1624.

Mus. Bac.—Michael Collard, who was required to compose a song of five parts, to be sung at the following Comitia.

Mus. Doc.—John Munday, of Christ Church. See p. 72.

1626.

Mus. Bac.—John Frith, Organist of St. John's Coll. He was required to compose a piece in seven parts for his degree. Wood had seen some of his compositions, but they do not appear to have been published. He died in 1644.‡

---

* Letter from Piers to Camden. Hawkins, p. 572, note.
† Fasti.   ‡ *Ibid.*

1629.

Mus. Bac. and Mus. Doc.—Mathew White, of Ch. Ch., accumulated the degrees. He was a bass singer at Wells Cathedral, and was Organist of Ch. Ch. from 1611 to 1613, then Gentleman of the Chapel Royal till 1614. He wrote some anthems, which are found in the Barnard MSS., Tudway, at Ely, and elsewhere.

1631.

Mus. Bac.—William Child, of Ch. Ch. He was born at Bristol about 1606, and educated under Elway Bevan, Organist of the Cathedral there. In 1630 he was appointed Lay Clerk and Organist of St. George's, Windsor, in conjunction with Nathaniel Giles, and in 1633 Organist of the Chapel Royal at Whitehall. During the Rebellion he retired to a small farm, where he occupied himself with composition. On the Restoration, he, together with Christopher Gibbons, Rogers, and others, set about re-organising the Cathedral service. He proceeded Mus. Doc. in 1663, and his exercise—an anthem—was performed at St. Mary's Church. He was Organist at St. George's, Windsor, Chamber Musician to Charles II., and Chanter of the King's Chapel. While he was at St. George's the salaries of the officers were very much in arrears, and Child, not expecting ever to see his, which amounted to some £500, said to one of the canons that he would be glad to take £5 and some bottles of wine for his arrears. The canons accepted this offer, and had sealed articles drawn up confirming the bargain. When James II. came to the throne, the arrears in the official salaries were paid off; but Dr. Child had lost all claim, owing to his bargain. The canons, however, released him, on condition of his promising to pave the choir of the Chapel, which he accordingly did, and it is recorded on his tombstone.* He died March 23, 1696-7, at the age of ninety, and was buried in St. George's Chapel. His compositions are "The first set of Psalms for III voyces," 1639; "Divine Anthems and other vocal compositions"; Catches in Hilton's "Catch who catch can," and some Court Ayres. His

---

* "Dict. Nat. Biog."

Church music is in Smith's " Musica Antiqua," in various Cathedrals, in the Tudway Collection, at the Fitzwilliam, Peterhouse, Christ Church, and the Music School, Oxford.

1633.

Mus. Bac.—John Okeover, of New College, Organist and Vicar-Choral of Wells Cathedral.

1638.

Mus. Bac. — Robert Lugge, Organist of St. John's. His Canticum in five parts was required to be sung in the Music School.

1639.

Mus. Bac.—William Ellis, Organist of Eton and afterwards of St. John's College, Oxford. He was expelled from the latter in the Rebellion, and made a living by holding weekly meetings for the practice of music at his house (*see* p. 47). Wood makes constant reference to these meetings, in which many of the best musicians of the day, such as Baltzar, Mell, Wilson, and others, took part. He published some rounds and canons in Hilton's Collection " Catch who catch can," 1652. After the Restoration, Ellis in all probability got back his appointment as Organist of St. John's, since he spent the rest of his life in Oxford, and, dying in 1674, was buried in Magdalen parish.

1640.

Mus. Bac.—Arthur Philipps, Organist of Magd. Coll. He succeeded Nicholson in 1639, under Dr. Heather's endowment, as the second Choragus, and retired in 1656. He was born in 1605; Clerk of New Coll., 1622; Organist of Bristol in 1638; Organist of Magdalen in 1639. Joining the Church of Rome, he went to France as Organist to Henrietta Maria, and after his return became Organist to Mr. Caryll, a gentleman living in Essex. His compositions are " The Requiem, or Liberty of an imprisoned Royalist," 1641, and " The Resurrection," 1649. Wood says that his vocal compositions had been tried and commended by several great masters of music.

F

1644-5.*

Mus. Doc.—John Wilson. Born at Faversham in 1594. He was a famous lute player. He was created Doctor of Music during the Royal residence at Oxford. On the surrender of the garrison of Oxford in 1646, he entered the family of Sir William Walter, of Sarsden, as Music-master. In 1656 he succeeded Philips as Professor† of Music, and held this post till 1662, when he became Chamber Musician to Charles II. and member of the Chapel Royal, in succession to Henry Lawes. He afterwards resided in London till his death, which took place at Westminster in 1673, and he was buried in the Cloisters. He is described by Wood as "the best at the lute in all England." He was a man of great humour, and was at one time supposed to be the Jack Wilson of Shakespeare. His compositions are some songs in "Select Musicall Ayres and dialogues," 1652, &c.; "Psalterium Carolinum, or the Devotions of His Sacred Majestie in his solitudes & sufferings" (1657), for three voices with organ or theorbo; "Cheerful Airs and Ballads," 1660; Services and Anthems, 1663; Music to some of the Odes of Horace, now in the Bodleian; a glee in praise of sack; and some songs in the British Museum. His compositions were for a long time in considerable favour.

1663.

Mus. Doc.—William Child, of Ch. Ch. *See* p. 80.

1664.

Mus. Doc.—Christopher Gibbons, of Christ Church, by Royal letters. He was born 1615, was a son of Orlando Gibbons, and was educated under his uncle, Ellis Gibbons, Organist of Exeter. In 1638 he became Organist of Winchester Cathedral. He was one of the few Church musicians left at the Restoration, and was at once made Organist of Westminster Abbey and the Chapel of Charles II. Wood says he was "a grand debauchee. He would often sleep at Morning Prayer when he was to play the organ."‡ The King

---

* Foster's "Alumni" gives the date as 1640-1.
† *I.e.*, Professor of the *Practical* part, or Choragus. The Lectureship had by this time been diverted from the intentions of its founder. *See* p. 35.
‡ "Wood's Life and Times." A. Clark, p. 5.

requested the University of Oxford to confer the degree of Doctor upon him, which was accordingly done in 1664, and his exercise was performed in St. Mary's Church "with very great honour to himself and his faculty."* Gibbons died in 1676. He excelled more as an organist than as a composer. His compositions are his "Act Song," performed for his degree, preserved in the Music School at Oxford; music to Shirley's Masque "Cupid and Death," composed in conjunction with Loch in 1653; some compositions in Playford's Cantica sacra, 1674; and some MSS. in the British and Fitzwilliam Museums.

1669.

Mus. Doc.—Benjamin Rogers, Organist of Magdalen, Bachelor of Music of Cambridge. *See* p. 128.

1682 (*circa*).

Mus. Bac.—About this date Richard Goodson, the elder, Organist of New Coll. and Ch. Ch., took his degree, and was in this year appointed Professor of Music. He died in 1718.

1707.

Mus. Bac.—Charles King, of Merton. He was born in 1687, was a chorister under Blow and J. Clark at St. Paul's, and succeeded the latter as Almoner and Master of the Choristers. In 1708 he was appointed Organist of St. Benet Fink, and in 1730 Vicar-Choral of St. Paul's. Some of his anthems are in Arnold's Cathedral Music, Page's Harmonia Sacra, and the Tudway Collection. He died in 1748.

1713.

Mus. Bac.—John Isham, or Isum, of Merton, was deputy to Croft, and going to Oxford to assist him in the performance of his Doctor's exercise, was himself admitted Mus. Bac., together with William Morley. Who his master was is not known. In 1711 he was elected Organist of St. Anne's, Westminster, in succession to Croft, and in 1718 Organist to St. Andrew's, Holborn, and afterwards of St. Margaret's, Westminster, which last he held till his death in 1726. His

---

* Fasti.

compositions are much praised by Hawkins, who gives a two-part song,* " Bury delights my roving eye." Other compositions are in a collection published by him in conjunction with Morley in 1710.

Mus. Bac.—William Morley, of Merton Coll. In 1715 he became a Gentleman of the Chapel Royal. His Chant in D minor in Boyce is supposed by some to be the earliest instance of a double chant. He died 1731.

Mus. Doc.—William Croft, of Christ Church. Born in 1677 or 1678, was a pupil of Dr. Blow† at the Chapel Royal. In 1700 he was appointed Organist of St. Anne's, Westminster, and resigned this post in 1711 in favour of John Isham. In 1700 he and Jeremiah Clark were sworn Gentlemen Extraordinary of the Chapel Royal, and in 1704 joint-Organists, in succession to Francis Piggott. In 1707 Croft became sole Organist at the Chapel Royal on Clark's death. In 1708 he succeeded Blow as Organist of Westminster Abbey, and Composer at the Chapel Royal, in which capacity it was his duty to produce anthems for State occasions. His degree exercise consisted of two Odes on the peace of Utrecht, written by Joseph Trapp. It was afterwards published under the title of "*Musicus Apparatus Academicus.*" In 1716 he was appointed tuner of the regals, an office which was abolished in 1773.‡ He was an original member of the Academy of Vocal Music, founded in 1725. He died in 1727, aged 50, and was buried at Westminster Abbey. His compositions are overtures and act tunes for " Courtship à la mode," produced 1700; the " Funeral and Twin Rivals," 1702; " The Lying Lover," 1703; Anthems written for State ceremonies, &c.; two folio volumes of sacred music, published 1724; six,

---

* Page 799.

† Blow is supposed to have been made Mus. Doc. by Archbishop Sancroft, about 1676; but a MS. Anthem formerly existing at the Oxford Music School, and now lost, suggests his having been an Oxford graduate. There is, however, no record of his having matriculated or entered his name at any College. (*See* " Dict. Nat. Biog.") Wood, in the Ashm. MSS., D. 4, speaks of him as Mus. Doc., Cantuar; and as they were contemporary, Wood ought to have known if he had graduated at Oxford.

‡ This was formerly an important office. Henry VIII.'s musical establishment contained thirteen single and five double regals. The regal was a portable organ, the sound of which being produced by "beating" reeds in very small pipes, the instrument required constant tuning. There are three or four regals at present in England, in private collections.

sonatas for two flutes; some songs, and six theatre airs. Some of his anthems are in the Tudway and other collections in the British Museum.

Mus. Doc.—Johan Christoph Pepusch, of Magd. Coll. Born at Berlin in 1667. At 14 years old he held an appointment at the Prussian Court. He devoted himself to the study of the Greek writers, and became a skilled theorist. He came to England about 1700, and played in the orchestra of Drury Lane, and also assisted in the production of the "Anglo-Italian" operas produced about 1707. He took an active part in the foundation of the Academy of Ancient Music in 1710. In 1712 he became Organist and Composer to the Duke of Chandos, at Cannons, for whom he composed and published several sets of Services and Anthems. His degree exercise was a setting of an Ode on the Peace of Utrecht. He revived the practice of solmisation by hexachords. About 1714 he became Music Director at Lincoln's Inn Fields Theatre, where he produced and arranged many masques, &c. In 1730 a "Treatise on Harmony" was published anonymously, containing the rules given by him, probably by his pupil, Viscount Paisley. In 1737 he was appointed Organist of the Charterhouse, where he spent the rest of his life. In 1746 he was elected F.R.S. He died in 1752. He produced, besides the compositions mentioned above, airs, sonatas, and concertos for various instruments, and some Latin motets. He bequeathed his library to John Travers and Ephraim Kelner, and on the death of the latter it was dispersed.

1716-17.

Mus. Bac.—Richard Goodson, the younger, of Ch. Ch., of which, together with New, he was Organist. He succeeded his father in these appointments, as well as that of Professor of Music in 1718. He died in 1741. His MSS., which are few in number, together with those of his father, are in the library of Ch. Ch. and the Music School.

1729.

Mus. Bac.—John Stanley. Born in 1713, he became blind at two years of age from an accident. He was a pupil of John Reading and Maurice Greene, and in 1724 was appointed

Organist of All Hallows', Bread Street, and, two years later, of St. Andrew's, Holborn. In 1739 he was appointed Organist of the Temple Church. He composed and produced the following Oratorios: "Jephthah," in 1757; "Zimri," 1760; and the "Fall of Egypt," 1774. He assisted in carrying on the Oratorio performances formerly conducted by Handel. In 1779 he succeeded Boyce as Master of the King's Band. He died in 1786. His compositions, besides those already mentioned, consist of six cantatas, for voice and instrument, three cantatas and three songs, three sets of organ voluntaries, and "Arcadia," a dramatic pastoral in honour of the marriage of George III.

1731.

Mus. Bac. and Mus. Doc.—Thomas Deane, Organist at Warwick and Coventry, who is said to have been the first to perform a sonata by Corelli in England, which he did in 1709. His compositions are a service and other Church music, incidental music to Oldmixon's "The Governor of Cyprus," and many contributions to the "Division Violin."

1735.

Mus. Bac.—William Hayes, Organist of Magd. Coll. Born in 1706,* he was taught the harpsichord by Mrs. Viney, and articled by her to W. Hine, Organist of Gloucester Cathedral. He became Organist of St. Mary's, Shrewsbury, in 1729, of Worcester Cathedral in 1731, and Magdalen College in 1734. He was Professor of Music from 1742 to 1777, and was created Mus. Doc. at the opening of the Radcliffe Library in 1749, on which occasion he directed the music. He was steward and conductor of the Worcester Festival in 1734. In 1763 he won three out of the four prizes first offered by the Glee Club. He died at Oxford in 1777. Hayes' compositions are English ballads, twelve arietts, and two cantatas, 1735; overture and songs in the "Masque of Circe"; a sonata or trio and ballad airs and cantatas; an Ode, being part of his Bachelor's exercise, 1765; instrumental accompaniments to the Old Hundredth Psalm,

---

* See "Dict. Nat. Biog."

1770; sixteen Psalms, from Merrick's version, 1775; Cathedral music, 1795; six cantatas, 1740 (?); Collins' "Ode to the Passions," 1775 (?).

Mus. Doc.—Maurice Greene, incorporated from Cambridge. *See* p. 132.

1749.
Mus. Doc.—William Hayes. *See* p. 86.

1755.
Mus. Bac.—John Alcock, or Allcock. Born 1715, was educated under Charles King, Organist of St. Paul's, and the blind Organist, John Stanley. In 1737 he was elected Organist of St. Andrew's, Plymouth. From 1742 to 1749 he was Organist of St. Lawrence, Reading. In the latter year he was appointed Organist, Vicar-Choral, and Master of the Choristers at Lichfield Cathedral. He proceeded Mus. Doc. in 1761 or 1765. From 1761 to 1786 he was Organist of Sutton Coldfield Parish Church, and from 1766 to 1790 of the Parish Church of Tamworth. He died at Lichfield, 1806. He was a composer of songs, solos for flute, harpsichord, and organ, besides Church music. He is described in the "Dictionary of National Biography" as "a thoroughly sound musician, . . . who preserved the traditions of the old English school of Church composers, free from the inanities in which some of his contemporaries indulged."

1757.
Mus. Bac.—William Walond, described as "Organorum pulsator," a member of Christ Church, took the degree of Bachelor of Music about this time. He published, about 1759, a setting of Pope's "St. Cecilia's Day."

1759.
Mus. Doc.—Thomas Augustine Arne. Born in 1710, was educated at Eton. Being obliged to conceal his love of music from his father, he privately took lessons from Michael Festing, the violinist, and practised on a spinet with muffled strings. He at the same time studied harmony and composition, and attended the opera in the disguise of a servant's livery. His father accidentally discovered him leading a

band of amateurs, and, after his first wrath was over, allowed him to give up the career of a lawyer, for which he had intended him, and devote himself to music. His first effort was music to Addison's "Rosamond," which was produced with considerable success at Lincoln's Inn Fields Theatre in 1733. This was followed by a number of operatic compositions and masques, including Milton's "Comus," performed at Drury Lane, 1738, which has kept the stage until comparatively recently; in 1740 "Alfred," a masque, was produced at Cliveden, Bucks, the residence of the Prince of Wales, in which the song "Rule, Brittania," occurs; in 1746 he wrote music for the "Tempest," at Drury Lane, in which is included the song "Where the bee sucks." In addition to taking high rank as a composer, he was excellent as a teacher of singing, his most successful pupil being Miss Brent, for whom he wrote a number of bravura airs. In 1755 and 1764 he produced his Oratorios "Abel" and "Judith," neither of which achieved any success. In 1760 Arne, being on bad terms with Garrick, left Drury Lane, of which the latter was manager, and transferred his services to Covent Garden, where he produced with success a translation of Metastasio's "Artaserse," with music in the style of the Italian opera of the day. After this he continued to produce light operas and incidental music for both Covent Garden and Drury Lane. In 1769 he set to music Garrick's Ode for the Jubilee of Shakespeare at Stratford-on-Avon. He died in 1778, and was buried at St. Paul's, Covent Garden. Most of his MSS. were destroyed at the fire of Covent Garden Theatre in 1808, but the score of "Judith" is at the British Museum.

Mus. Doc.—John Buswell, incorporated from Cambridge. *See* p. 135.

1761.

Mus. Bac.—Richard Langdon, Organist and Sub-Chanter of Exeter Cathedral and afterwards Organist of Bristol Cathedral. In 1782 he was appointed Organist of Armagh Cathedral. He published a collection of Psalms and Anthems in score, entitled "Divine Harmony," in 1774. His other publications are twelve glees, two books of songs, and some canzonets. Warren's "Vocal Harmony" contains some of his compositions. His Double Chant in F is well known. He died in 1803.

Mus. Doc.—John Alcock proceeded either this year or in 1765. See p. 87.

1763.

Mus. Bac.—Philip Hayes, of Magd. Coll., son of William Hayes, was Organist of Ch. Ch. from 1763 to 1765; Gentleman of the Chapel Royal, 1767: Organist of New College, in succession to Richard Church, 1776, and Magdalen, 1777, in which year he succeeded his father as Professor of Music and proceeded Mus. Doc. He became Organist of St. John's College in 1790, in succession to Thomas Norris, and died in London suddenly in 1797, and was buried at St. Paul's. He was extremely corpulent, and was supposed to be the largest man in England.* Among his compositions are six Concertos for organ, harpsichord, or pianoforte, 1769; eight Anthems, 1780; "Prophecy," an Oratorio, performed at Oxford, 1781;† catches, glees, canons, 1785; an "Ode," performed at Cambridge, 1785; catches and glees, 1789; "Ode for St. Cecilia's Day," by John Oldham; "Telemachus," a masque, and a number of single anthems, songs, and glees.

1765.

Mus. Bac.—Thomas Norris. Born about 1745, was educated under Stephens at Salisbury Cathedral. He was appointed Organist of Ch. Ch. in 1765. His degree exercise, which consisted of two Anthems, "The Lord is King" and "I will always give thanks," was performed in the Music School. He was also appointed Organist of St. John's College in 1765. In 1771 he became a Lay-Clerk of Magd. Coll., Oxford. He died in 1790, through over-exertion at the Birmingham Festival. He was an excellent tenor singer, in which capacity he was engaged for the Gloucester and Three Choirs Festivals, at the Handel Commemoration in 1784, and for the Oratorios in London. He composed several anthems, six symphonies for strings, two hautboys, and two horns,‡ some glees, canons, and other vocal pieces.

---

* Bloxam, "Reg. Magd. Coll.," II., 220.   † See p. 33.
‡ Many of Haydn's early symphonies are for this combination of instruments.

1766.

Mus. Bac.—John Alcock, the younger son of John Alcock the elder, born about 1740. He was Organist successively of St. Mary Magdalen, Newark-on-Trent, and the Parish Church at Walsall. He died in 1791. He published several songs, anthems, lessons, and sonatas for harpsichord and for strings.

1769.

Mus. Doc.—Charles Burney, author of the "History of Music." Born in 1726, he studied music under his half-brother, James, Organist of St. Mary's, Shrewsbury, and Baker, Organist of Chester Cathedral, and, finally, under Arne, in London. While under the tuition of Arne he contributed some of the music to Thomson's "Alfred," produced at Drury Lane in 1745. In 1747 he published six sonatas for two violins and bass. He was afterwards introduced by Kirkman, the piano-maker, to Fulke Greville, who paid Arne £300 to cancel his articles and took Burney to live with him. In 1749 he was appointed Organist of St. Dionis, Backchurch, and Conductor of the "New Concerts" at the King's Arms, Cornhill. Having a severe illness, he was ordered to quit London, and became Organist of Lynn Regis about 1750. During his nine years' residence there he formed plans for his future "History of Music." In 1760, on the restoration of his health, he returned to London and settled in Poland Street as a teacher. In 1769 he took the degree of Mus. Doc., his exercise being so successful that it was repeated several times, and also performed at Hamburg under C. P. E. Bach. About this time he devoted much time to astronomical pursuits, which brought on another attack of illness. Having recovered, in 1770 he left England with letters of introduction to influential persons, and travelled to Italy to collect material for his history. The account of his tour was published in 1771. In 1772 he travelled in Germany and Netherlands, and an account of this tour was published in 1773, in which year he was made a Fellow of the Royal Society. In 1776 the first volume of his history appeared, dedicated to Queen Charlotte. The second volume appeared in 1782, the third and fourth in 1789. The work was very successful from the first, but posterity has decided in favour of Hawkins' similar work. In 1774 he formed a plan for the establishment of a Music School in England on the Italian system, which was, however, not realised. In 1783 he was appointed Organist of Chelsea Hospital. In 1796, after another attack of illness, he published a life of Metastasio. In 1806 Fox gave him a pension of £300. In 1810 he was made a member of the Institut de France. He died in 1814, after a long and most active life, and was buried at Chelsea Hospital. Besides his various literary productions, of which only the most important are mentioned above, he was a composer of concertos and sonatas for organ, harpsichord, and string instruments, as well as cantatas and songs.

1773.

Mus. Bac. and Mus. Doc.—Samuel Arnold was offered these degrees by the University, and was asked to allow his Oratorio " The Prodigal Son " to be performed for the installation of Lord North as Chancellor. Arnold, however, declined the offer, saying he wished to take the degree in the ordinary way. On his sending his exercise to Dr. Hayes, the Professor, the latter returned it unopened, saying that it was unnecessary to examine an exercise by the composer of " The Prodigal Son." Arnold was born in 1740, and was educated at the Chapel Royal under Nares and Gates. In 1773 he was engaged by Beard as composer to Covent Garden, and in 1775 brought out the " Maid of the Mill," the first of a long series of pasticcios.* He also composed several Oratorios. In 1769 and the succeeding three years he lost £10,000 over the production of operas and burlettas at Marylebone Gardens. In 1783 he succeeded Nares as Organist and Composer to the Chapel Royal. In 1786 he undertook an edition of Handel's works, at the request of George III. In 1790 the " Graduates' Meeting," a Society of Musical Professors established in London, was founded at Arnold's house.† In the same year he published his

---

* Pasticcios were so-called dramas, consisting of a number of airs and duets, &c., gathered from various operas and composers, and strung together without any other design than that of giving a mixed audience a succession of popular airs.   † *See* Appendix U.

Cathedral music. In 1793 he succeeded Dr. Cooke as Organist of Westminster Abbey. He died in 1802 from injuries received through a fall from his library steps, and was buried in Westminster Abbey, next to Purcell.

1774.

Mus. Bac. and Mus. Doc.—Robert Wainwright, of Magdalen College.* Born in 1748; Organist of St. Peter's, Liverpool, 1775. His Oratorio "The Fall of Egypt" was produced at Liverpool in 1780, and he wrote some services and anthems. He died in 1782.

1777.

Mus. Bac. and Mus. Doc.—John Abraham Fisher. Born in 1744. He was taught the violin by Pinto, under the patronage of Lord Tyrawley. He first appeared at the King's Theatre in 1763, where he played a concerto. In 1764 he became a member of the Royal Society of Musicians. His degree exercise, "Providence," an Oratorio, was performed in the Sheldonian Theatre. In 1770 he became entitled, through his wife, to a sixteenth share in Covent Garden Theatre, to which Institution he accordingly devoted all his talent and energy. About 1784 he made a professional tour in France, Germany, and Russia. In Vienna three languages were employed by the Tonkünstler-Societät to describe him : "Monsieur Fischer, ein Engelländer und virtuoso di violino."† The Emperor Joseph ordered him to quit his dominion in consequence of his ill-treatment of, and separation from, his second wife, Anna Storace. He therefore went to Dublin, where he gave concerts and taught the violin till his death in 1806. He wrote various music for the violin, some songs, six symphonies, theatrical music, and an Anthem, "Seek ye the Lord," sung at Bedford Chapel and Lincoln Cathedral.

Mus. Doc.—Philip Hayes. *See* p. 89.

---

* Foster, "Alumni."
† "Dict. Nat. Biog."

1785.

Mus. Bac.—John Wall Callcott, of Magd. Hall. Born at Kensington in 1766. He first studied music under Henry Whitney, Organist of Kensington Parish Church. He was Deputy-Organist of St. George-the-Martyr, Bloomsbury, from 1783 to 1785, in which year he took his Mus. Bac. degree, his exercise being a setting of Warton's " Ode to Fancy." His compositions frequently won prizes at the Catch Club competitions, and in one year he sent in 100 compositions, only two of which, however, were successful. In 1789 he and C. S. Evans were appointed joint-Organists of St. Paul's, Covent Garden. In 1791 he studied under Haydn, and wrote a symphony under his guidance. From 1793 to 1802 he was Organist of the Asylum for Female Orphans. He proceeded Mus. Doc. in 1800, his exercise being the Anthem " Propter Sion non tacebo." His Musical Grammar, published in 1806, was very successful, and he was this year appointed Lecturer at the Royal Institution in succession to Dr. Crotch, but his brain gave way in 1807, necessitating his removal to an asylum. He died in 1821, and was buried at Kensington. Callcott composed many glees, catches, and canons—some of which were published by Horsley, his son-in-law, in 1824—some sacred trios, anthems, and hymns, and six sonatas for the harpsichord.

1788.

Mus. Doc.—Edmund Ayrton is said to have incorporated from Cambridge, but it is doubtful if he did so.* *See* p. 137.

1789.

Mus. Doc.—Frederick Hartmann Graff (called by Fétis, Fredéric Hermann Graf). He was chief musician in the Church of Augsburg, and a member of the Royal University of Music at Stockholm. Born at Rudolstadt, 1727. Was an excellent flautist. In 1783 he came to London to direct the grand concerts just established there.† After this he went to

---

* Foster, "Alumni."
† These concerts took place at Hanover Square Rooms. The programme of the first (on February 19, 1783) contains two concertos by Graff; one for flute, hautbois, clarionet, horn, and bassoon; the other for violin, flute, and tenor.— *Morning Chronicle*, February 19, 1783.

Augsburg as Capellmeister. He was created Mus. Doc. at Oxford as a token of the great appreciation the English nation had of his talent. He died 1795, aged 68. He published a large number of pieces for the flute, and left others in MS., besides some Oratorios.—*Fétis*.

1790.

Mus. Bac. and Mus. Doc.—Thomas Sanders Dupuis. Born in 1733, of a Huguenot family; was brought up as a chorister of the Chapel Royal, under Bernard Gates and John Travers. He was appointed Organist of Charlotte Street (now St. Peter's) Chapel, near Buckingham Palace, in 1773, and succeeded Boyce at the Chapel Royal as Organist and Composer in 1779. In 1790, the year in which he took his degrees, he formed the "Graduates' Meeting" for purposes of social intercourse between musicians resident in London.* He died in 1796, and was buried in Westminster Abbey. A collection of his Cathedral Music was published by his pupil, John Spencer. He was an excellent organist.

1791.

Mus. Doc.—Joseph Haydn was created Doctor of Music at Dr. Burney's suggestion. He wrote a new Symphony as his exercise, but, owing to the lack of time for rehearsals, the one in G, known as the "Oxford Symphony," was substituted. It was performed at the second of three grand concerts, and Haydn conducted at the organ. At the third concert he appeared in his Doctor's robes, amid enthusiastic applause.† In addition to the Symphony, he sent as an exercise a "Canon cancrizans a tre" to the words "Thy voice, O Harmony, is divine."

Mus. Bac. and Mus. Doc.—Theodore Aylward, of Magd. Coll. Born in 1730. Nothing is known of his early life. He became a member of the Royal Society of Musicians in 1763, and Organist of St. Lawrence, Jewry, in 1762, which post he held simultaneously with the organistship of St. Michael's, Cornhill, from 1768. In 1771 he was elected

---

* Appendix U.   † Grove's Dict.

Professor of Music at Gresham College, and in 1788 Organist of St. George's Chapel, Windsor, in succession to Edward Webb. He died in 1801, and was buried in St. George's Chapel. His music is still in MS., except a few songs, duets, glees, and organ pieces.

Mus. Bac.—Clement Smith. He matriculated at Magd. College, and proceeded Mus. Doc. from Magd. Hall in 1800.

Mus. Bac.—John Hindle. Matriculated at Magd. Coll., and probably graduated as Mus. Bac. this year. He was Lay-Vicar of Westminster Abbey, and composed some songs, glees, and a well-known chant. He died in 1796.

1792.

Mus. Bac.—Joseph William Holder. Born in 1794, and educated under Dr. Nares at the Chapel Royal. He was Assistant-Organist at St. George-the-Martyr, Queen's Square, under Reinthaler, and afterwards held appointments at Bungay and Chelmsford. The score of his degree exercise, an Anthem, is in the Music School. He composed a mass and some anthems, glees, songs, canons, and pianoforte pieces. He died in 1832.

1793.

Mus. Bac.—John Clarke, afterwards Clarke-Whitfeld. He was born in 1770, and educated at Oxford under Dr. Philip Hayes. He was appointed Organist of Armagh Cathedral in 1794, having been in the previous year appointed Master of the Choristers of St. Patrick's and Christ Church, Dublin. He graduated as Doctor of Music at Dublin in 1795. In 1798, being driven out of Dublin by the Rebellion, he became Organist of Trinity and St. John's Colleges, Cambridge. In 1799 he took the Degree of Doctor of Music at Cambridge, and in 1810 incorporated at Oxford. In 1820 he was appointed Organist of Hereford Cathedral, and in 1821 Professor of Music at Cambridge. He died in 1836, and was buried at Hereford Cathedral. His compositions consist of "The Resurrection," an Oratorio, glees, songs, &c., and Cathedral services and anthems. He also edited a collection of thirty Anthems, and arranged several of Handel's Oratorios for voices and pianoforte.

1794.

Mus. Bac.—William Crotch, of St. Mary Hall, took this degree at the age of eighteen. He was born in 1775, and at two years and three weeks old could play "God save the Queen" and a few other tunes on a small organ built by his father, who was a carpenter. In 1779 he was announced as "The Musical Child, who will perform of the organ every day as usual from one o'clock, till three, at Mrs. Hart's, Milliner, Piccadilly." In 1782 he could play the violin, as well as the organ and pianoforte. In 1786 he went to Cambridge as assistant and pupil to Dr. Randall. In 1789 an Oratorio, "The Captivity of Judah," by him, was performed at Trinity Hall, Cambridge. He was also engaged this year to play concertos at the weekly concerts in the Oxford Music Room. In 1790 he succeeded Thomas Norris as Organist of Christ Church, and in 1797 he succeeded Dr. Hayes as Organist of St. John's, St. Mary's Church, and Professor of Music at Oxford. He proceeded Mus. Doc. in 1799, his exercise being a setting of Warton's "Ode to Fancy," which he published in 1800. He delivered courses of lectures during the next four years at Oxford. About 1810 he removed to London, where he occupied himself with teaching. In 1812 his famous Oratorio "Palestine" was produced at Hanover Square Rooms, and in the same year he published his "Elements of Musical Composition." In 1820 he lectured at the Royal Institution, and composed an Ode on the accession of George IV., which was performed at Oxford. He was the first Principal of the Royal Academy of Music, founded in 1822. In 1834 he produced a second Oratorio, "The Captivity of Judah" (distinct from his early work of that name), at Oxford for the installation of the Duke of Wellington as Chancellor. His last public appearance was at the Handel Festival of 1834, at Westminster Abbey, where he played the organ on June 28. He died December 29, 1847, and was buried at Bishop's Hall, near Taunton. Being mainly dependent on teaching for a livelihood, he was unable to devote much time to composition. "He was a learned musician, but not a dry one, and probably, if he had lived in a more congenial musical atmosphere, would have attained a far higher standard than he did."*

1797.

Mus. Bac.—George Baker is supposed to have taken this degree. He was born about 1773, and educated at Exeter, under Hugh Bond and William Jackson. Under the patronage of the Earl of Uxbridge, he became a pupil of Cramer and Dussek. In 1794 or 1795 he was appointed Organist of St. Mary's Church, Stafford. In the books of the church are entries which show an unsatisfactory state of affairs, such as that he was prohibited from playing his piece called "The Storm," that he was restricted as to his use of the organ, and that he habitually neglected his duties. He became Organist of All Saints', Derby, in 1810, and of Rugeley in 1824, where he died in 1847. His compositions, of which he produced a large quantity, are now completely forgotten. He laid claim to the degree of Mus. Doc., and is thus described in Grove's Dictionary, but there is no record of his having taken this degree at Oxford or Cambridge.†

Mus. Bac.—Jacob Cubitt Pring. Born in 1771, was Organist of St. Botolph, Aldgate. He composed anthems and glees, and was one of the founders of the "Concentores Sodales."‡ He died in 1799.

1799.

Mus. Bac.—Isaac Pring. Born in 1777, brother of Jacob and Joseph. He and his brothers were all choristers at St. Paul's, under Hudson. He was Assistant-Organist to Dr. Philip Hayes, and, on his death, succeeded him as Organist of New College. He died in 1799 of consumption.

Mus. Bac.—Jeremiah Clarke matriculated at Magd. Hall, and probably took the degree of Mus. Bac. He was born about 1750, and educated as a chorister at Worcester, under Elias Isaac. His name appears as a violinist at most of the Birmingham Festivals and Concerts from 1764. In 1806 he became Organist of Worcester and, in consequence, Conductor of the Three Choirs Festival.§ He died in

---

* "Dict. Nat. Biog." † See "Dict. Nat. Biog." ‡ *See* p. 98.
§ Lyson's Annals of the Three Choirs. Ed. of 1812, p. 231. "Since this time (1790) the music has been uniformly conducted by the Organists of the respective Cathedrals."

1809. His compositions include songs with orchestra, harpsichord sonatas with string accompaniments, glees, and a set of instructions for singers.

Mus. Doc.—William Crotch. *See* p. 96.

1800.

Mus. Bac.—William Horsley. Born 1774. He was trained under Theodore Smith, the brothers Pring, and J. W. Callcott. In 1794 he became Organist of Ely Chapel, Holborn, and in 1798 founded, in conjunction with Callcott, a club for the encouragement of glee and canon writing, called the "Concentores Sodales," which existed till about 1847. His exercise was an anthem, "When Israel came out of Egypt." In 1802 he succeeded Callcott as Organist to the Asylum for Female Orphans, of which he had for some time been acting as Assistant-Organist. He was one of the founders of the Philharmonic Society in 1813. In 1838 he became Organist of the Charterhouse. He was elected a member of the Royal Academy of Music of Stockholm in 1847. He died in 1858. His reputation as a composer rests chiefly on his glees, of which Mendelssohn had a very high opinion, and in which form of writing he has had few equals. At one time Mendelssohn found that, during his absence from Leipsic, the Sing-Verein had made the mistake of performing Horsley's glee "By Celia's Arbour," with forty voices to a part. Besides glees, he published some works on theory, some hymn and Psalm tunes, songs, and piano pieces, and edited Callcott's Musical Grammar, some of his glees, and part of Bird's "*Cantiones Sacræ.*"

Mus. Doc.—John Wall Callcott. *See* p. 93.

Mus. Doc.—Clement Smith, Magd. Hall. *See* p. 95.

1803.

Mus. Bac. and Mus. Doc.—John Christmas Beckwith, of Magd. Hall. He was born in 1759, and was a pupil of Drs. W. and P. Hayes. In 1794 he became Organist of St. Peter Mancrofts, Norwich, and in 1808 succeeded T. Garland as Organist of Norwich Cathedral. He died 1809. His compositions consist of anthems, organ voluntaries, a concerto, a sonata, &c., and a collection of chants. He was an organist of very high rank, with remarkable power of extemporising, and would frequently play four extempore fugues in one service.

1805.

Mus. Bac.—Walter Vicary, Organist of Magdalen College, 1797-1845; Lay-Chaplain of New College, 1812-44; Singing Man of St. John's College, 1816-28; Organist of St. Mary's Church, 1830. He was born in 1770, and died in 1845.

1806.

Mus. Bac.—Timothy Essex, of Magd. Hall. Born about 1765. In 1786 he established himself at Coventry as music teacher. He proceeded Mus. Doc. 1812, about which time he was Organist and Choirmaster of St. George's Chapel, Albemarle Street, near which he had established a Musical Academy. His compositions consist of English canzonets, music for pianoforte and violin, an organ fugue, and a collection of melodies for the Psalms, besides marches, rondos, and songs. He died in 1847.

Mus. Bac.—William Woodcock, of New Coll. Born 1754, Organist and Singing Man of New Coll., 1799-1825; Clerk of Magd. Coll., 1784-1818. He died in 1825.

1808.

Mus. Bac.—William Russell matriculated at Magd. Hall, and probably took this degree. He was born in 1777, and was a pupil of Cope, Shrubsole, and Groombridge, Organists of London churches. In 1793 he became Organist of the Chapel in Great Queen Street, Lincoln's Inn Fields. He was afterwards a pupil of Dr. Arnold. In 1798 he was appointed Organist of St. Ann's, Limehouse, and in 1800 pianist and composer at Sadler's Wells. In 1801 he became Organist of the Foundling Hospital. He composed two Oratorios, four odes, several glees, songs, organ voluntaries, and about twenty dramatic pieces. He died in 1813.

Mus. Bac. and Mus. Doc.—Joseph Pring. Born 1776, brother of Jacob Cubitt (p. 97). Organist of Bangor Cathedral. He was for several years engaged in a lawsuit to recover certain tithes belonging to the maintenance of the Cathedral choir, which had been diverted to other purposes, in which he was only partially successful. He published a history of these transactions in 1819. He died in 1842.

1810.

Mus. Doc.—John Clarke-Whitfeld. Incorporated from Cambridge. *See* p. 95.

1812.

Mus. Bac.—John Jeremiah Jones, Magd. Hall, a pupil of Crotch, and composer of a set of Six Fugues for the organ, some Songs, Ballads, and Glees.

Mus. Bac.—William Henry Cutler, Magd. Hall. Born in 1792. Chorister of St. Paul's, and pupil of William Russell. His exercise was an anthem, which he afterwards published. In 1818 he became Organist of St. Helen's, Bishopsgate, and in 1821 appeared as a singer at Drury Lane Theatre. In 1823 he became Organist of Quebec Chapel, Portman Square. His compositions are anthems, a service, songs, and pianoforte pieces. He gave a grand concert at the Opera House in 1824, and after this disappears from history.

Mus. Doc.—Timothy Essex, Magd. Hall. *See* p. 99.

1814.

Mus. Bac.—Joseph McMurdie, Magd. Hall. Born in 1792. A pupil of Dr. Crotch. He composed many glees and songs, of which the best known is the glee " By the dark rolling waters." He was also the author of works on harmony and psalmody. He was for more than thirty years a Director of the Philharmonic Society. He died in 1878.

1825.

Mus. Bac.—Alfred Bennett, who became Organist of New Coll. and the University in 1825. He published a service, some anthems, and a collection of chants. He died in 1830, at the age of twenty-five.

1826.

Mus. Bac.—William Marshall, of Ch. Ch.* Born in 1806, and educated at the Chapel Royal, under J. Stafford Smith and William Hawes. He was appointed Organist of Ch. Ch. and St. John's College in 1823, proceeded Mus. Doc. in 1840, and in 1846 became Organist of St. Mary's, Kidderminster. He died in 1875. His publications are "The Art of Reading Church Music" (1842), an edition of some chants, and a book of words of anthems.

1831.

Mus. Bac.—Stephen Elvey, of New Coll. Born in 1805, and educated at Canterbury Cathedral, under Highmore Skeats. He succeeded A. Bennett as Organist of New Coll. in 1830, and proceeded Mus. Doc. in 1838. He was Organist of St. Mary's Church and St. John's College, and deputy to Crotch as Professor of Music and Choragus. Crotch died in 1848 and Elvey succeeded him as Choragus, Sir H. Bishop being appointed Professor of Music. He died in 1860. His compositions are an Evening Service in continuation of Crotch's Morning Service in A, and six original tunes in the Oxford Psalm Book, 1852. He also published "Psalter and Canticles, pointed for Chanting."

1833.

Mus. Bac.—W. Dawson Littledale, Brasenose.
Mus. Bac.—James Harris, Magd. Hall.
Mus. Doc.—Benjamin Blyth, Magd. Hall. Published some songs and Church music. His son was afterwards Organist of Magdalen.

1838.

Mus. Bac.—George Job Elvey, New College. Mus. Doc., 1840; knighted 1871.
Mus. Doc.—Stephen Elvey, New College.

---

* The "Alumni Oxonienses" (Foster) gives 1826 as the date that W. Marshall took his degree, while Grove's Dictionary gives 1836, probably by a printer's error.

1839.

Mus. Bac.—Henry Rowley Bishop, of Magdalen College. Born in 1786. Was taught music by Francesco Bianchi. His first compositions were a set of twelve glees and some Italian songs. His first opera, "Angelina," was performed at Margate, 1804. In 1806 the success of his "Tamerlan et Bajazet," at the King's Theatre, led to his engagement at that house, and he produced a mass of compilations, arrangements, and incidental music. His first important opera, "The Circassian Bride," was produced at Drury Lane on February 23, 1809, with great success, but on the following night the theatre was burnt. He was one of the original members of the Philharmonic Society on its foundation in 1813. He was engaged in 1810, and for many years afterwards, at Covent Garden Theatre, where he produced a large number of operas, including "The Libertine," a free adaptation of Mozart's "Don Juan." In 1820 he went to Dublin, where he was received with great honour, and the freedom of the city was bestowed on him. In 1826 he was commissioned to write a grand opera, on the subject of "Aladdin," for Drury Lane, as a counter-attraction to Weber's "Oberon" at Covent Garden. In 1830 he was appointed Musical Director at Vauxhall Gardens. In 1832 he wrote a sacred cantata, "The Seventh Day," for the Philharmonic Society. He was a Professor of Harmony and Composition at the Royal Academy of Music, and in 1841 was elected Reid Professor of Music at Edinburgh, which post he held till 1843, when he was succeeded by Henry Hugo Pierson. In 1842 he was knighted by the Queen, this being the first occasion on which a musician had been thus honoured. In 1848 he was made Professor of Music at Oxford in succession to Crotch, and in 1853 he became a Doctor of Music, on the occasion of the installation of the Earl of Derby as Chancellor, for which he wrote an Ode as his exercise. In his old age he suffered from pecuniary difficulties, and complained of the neglect of the public, whose slave he acknowledged he had been. In the Liverpool Free Library are MSS. of "additional accompaniments" to, and alterations made by him in, the works of Beethoven, Mozart, Cherubini, and others, to suit public taste! His own style of composition is based on that of his master, Bianchi. His best works are his glees. He died in 1855 of cancer, and was buried at the Marylebone Cemetery, in which a monument was raised to him by public subscription. His MS. scores are preserved in the British Museum, the Royal College of Music, and in the Free Library of Liverpool.

Mus. Bac. and Mus. Doc.—Samuel Sebastian Wesley, son of Samuel and grandson of Rev. Charles Wesley. He was born in 1810, and educated at the Bluecoat School. He became a chorister of the Chapel Royal, St. James's, in 1813, and in 1827 was appointed Organist of St. James's Church, Hampstead. Shortly after this he was holding four organ appointments simultaneously. In 1832 he became Organist of Hereford Cathedral, and was Conductor of the Festival of 1834. In 1835 he was appointed Organist of Exeter Cathedral, at which time he was considered the first organist and church composer in England. In 1842 he became Organist of Leeds Parish Church, and in 1849 of Winchester Cathedral. His degree exercise was the eight-part anthem "O Lord, Thou art my God." In 1865 he was appointed Organist of Gloucester Cathedral, where he remained till his death in 1876. His compositions consist of anthems, services, glees, organ and piano pieces, of which a catalogue is given in Grove's Dictionary.

Mus. Bac.—George French Flowers, Lincoln College. Born in 1811, was a pupil of C. H. Rinck and Schnyder von Wartensee, and became Organist of the English Chapel at Paris. He was afterwards Organist of St. Mark's Church, Myddelton Square, and critic of the *Literary Gazette*. He proceeded Doctor of Music in 1865. He died in 1872 of cholera. He published an "Essay on the construction of Fugue," with an introduction containing new rules on harmony, music to Tennyson's "Ode on the Death of Wellington," and other vocal pieces. He was also a successful teacher of singing.

1840.

Mus. Doc.—William Marshall, of Ch. Ch. *See* p. 101.
Mus. Doc.—George Job Elvey, of Magd. Coll. *See* p. 101.

1842.

Mus. Bac.—Kellow John Pye.

1845.

Mus. Bac.—Benjamin Long, of New College.
Mus. Bac.—Edward Redhead, of Magd. Coll.

1846.

Mus. Bac.—William Richard Bexfield, of New College. Born in 1824, was a pupil of Dr. Zechariah Buck,* and Organist of Boston Church. He lectured on music, and was a candidate for the Oxford Professorship in 1848, in which year he became Organist of St. Helen's, Bishopsgate Street. In 1849 he proceeded Doctor of Music at Cambridge, and in 1852 his Oratorio "Israel restored" was produced at Norwich Festival. He died in 1853, at the age of twenty-nine. Some organ fugues and anthems by him were published after his death.

1847.

Mus. Bac.—Charles William Corfe, of Christ Church. Born in 1814, son of A. T. Corfe, the Organist of Salisbury. In 1846 he became Organist of Christ Church, and in 1860 Choragus of the University. He proceeded Mus. Doc. in 1852. He died in 1883. His compositions consist of glees, anthems, part-songs, &c.

Mus. Bac.—Charles Goodban, of Magd. Hall. Born in 1812, composer of some miscellaneous pieces. He died in 1881.

1848.

Mus. Bac.—Thomas I'ons, or Irons, of Magdalen College. Was born in 1817. He proceeded Mus. Doc. in 1854; died in 1857. He was the composer of anthems, glees, and songs, and Editor of "*Cantica ecclesiastica*," a collection of hymn tunes and chants.

Mus. Bac.—John Sewell, of Magd. Hall. Mus. Doc., 1856.

Mus. Bac.—Edwin George Monk, of Exeter Coll. Mus. Doc., 1856.

---

* Zechariah Buck, Mus. Doc., Cantuar, 1853. Born in 1799, died 1879. He was for many years Organist of Norwich Cathedral, and had a great reputation as a teacher.

1850.

Mus. Bac.—Sir Frederick Arthur Gore Ouseley, Bart., Christ Church. Born 1825, the son of the Right Hon. Sir Gore Ouseley, Bart., Ambassador to the Courts of Persia and St. Petersburg. His skill in music developed very early, and at eight years old he composed an opera, "L'Isola disabitata." He graduated B.A., 1846; M.A., 1849; Mus. Bac., 1850; Mus. Doc., 1854, in which year he succeeded Sir H. Bishop as Professor of Music, and was ordained and appointed Precentor of Hereford Cathedral. In 1856 he became Vicar of St. Michael's, Tenbury, and Warden of St. Michael's College for the education of boys in music and general knowledge, an establishment which he founded and maintained. He took a high rank as a performer on the organ and piano, and his extempore fugal playing was unsurpassed in England. As Professor of Music he introduced many reforms and improvements in the degree system, and raised the standard of the requirements, adopting, amongst other things, the preliminary examination in general knowledge which had been originated by Sir Robert Stewart at Dublin. He died in 1889. His compositions consist of upwards of seventy anthems, many services, organ music, glees and part-songs, solo songs, and two string quartets and two oratorios. He also published standard works on harmony, canon and fugue, and form and general composition.

1850.

Mus. Bac.—Charles Hackett, Magd. Hall.

Mus. Bac.—William Peregrine Propert, of Jesus.

1852.

Mus. Bac.—John Fawcett. Born about 1824. At eleven years old was appointed Organist of Farnworth. Studied at the Royal Academy of Music under Sterndale Bennett, during which time he was Organist of Curzon Street Chapel. The exercise for his degree, a cantata, "Supplication and Thanksgiving," was highly commended by Sir H. Bishop, the then Professor. Fawcett died at Manchester in 1857.

Mus. Bac.—Symeon Grosvenor, Magd. Hall.

Mus. Bac.—George Benjamin Allen, Magd. Hall.

Mus. Bac.—George Dixon, Magd. Hall. Born at Norwich, 1820. Pupil of Dr. Buck as a chorister of Norwich Cathedral; Organist successively of the Parish Churches of Retford, Louth, and Grantham from 1865 to 1886; Mus. Doc., 1858. Died 1887. Composer of several anthems, hymn tunes, chants, kyries, &c., some songs, and two cantatas.

Mus. Doc.—Charles William Corfe, Ch. Ch. *See* p. 104.

1854.

Mus. Bac.—Walter Bond Gilbert, Magd. Hall. Mus. Doc., 1888.
Mus. Bac.—William Taylor, Magd. Hall.
Mus. Bac.—James Petch, New Coll., Mus. Doc., Cantuar, 18—.
Mus. Doc.—Sir Henry Rowley Bishop. *See* p. 102.
Mus. Doc.—The Rev. Sir F. A. G. Ouseley, Bart. *See* p. 105.
Mus. Doc.—Thomas I'ons. *See* p. 104.

1855.

Mus. Bac.—Charles Frederick Hempel, Magd. Hall. Born 1811, educated by his father, the Organist of St. Mary's Church, Truro. He published songs, piano and dance music. Succeeded his father as Organist of St. Mary's, Truro, in 1844. Proceeded Mus. Doc., 1862, his exercise being an Oratorio, "The Seventh Seal." In 1857 he was appointed Organist of St. John's Episcopal Church, Perth, where he died in 1867.

Mus. Bac.—George Benjamin Arnold, New College. Mus. Doc., 1861.

Mus. Bac.—(Rev.) Richard Haking, Worcester College. Mus. Doc., 1864.

1856.

Mus. Bac.—(Rev.) Leighton George Hayne, Queen's College. Born in 1836. Organist of Queen's, 1857; Mus. Doc., 1860; Precentor of Queen's, 1860; Coryphæus of the University, 1863. He was appointed Vicar of Helston in 1866 and Rector of Mistley in 1871. Succentor of Eton from 1867 to 1871. He died in 1883.

Mus. Bac.—Stephen Georgeson Hatherley, New Coll.

1858.

Mus. Bac.—Philip Armes, New Coll. Mus. Doc., 1864; Mus. Bac., Durham, 1863; Mus. Doc., Durham, 1874.

Mus. Bac.—James Russell, Magd. Hall. Mus. Doc., 1865.
Mus. Doc.—George Dixon, Magd. Hall. *See* p. 106.

1859.
Mus. Bac.—Frederick Pyke Atkins, Magd. Hall.
Mus. Bac.—Stephen Austen Pearce, New Coll. Mus. Doc., 1864.
Mus. Bac.—Richard Boyer Sankey, Magd. Hall. B.A. and M.A., 1865.
Mus. Bac.—John Stainer, Christ Church. B.A., 1863; M.A., 1866; Mus. Doc., 1865; Knighted, 1888; Professor of Music, in succession to Sir F. A. G. Ouseley, 1889.

1860.
Mus. Bac.—Stephen James Pearce, New Coll.
Mus. Bac.—William Pole, F.R.S., St. John's College. Mus. Doc., 1867.
Mus. Doc.—Leighton George Hayne, Queen's Coll. *See* p. 106.

1861.
Mus. Bac.—Robert Sloman, Christ Church. Mus. Doc., 1867.
Mus. Doc.—George Benjamin Arnold, New Coll.

1862.
Mus. Bac.—Edward Herbert, Magd. Hall. Born 1830. Organist of Perth Cathedral, and afterwards of Sherborne Abbey Church. Died 1872. Composer of some anthems, and author of a Manual on the Rudiments of Music.
Mus. Bac.—Henry Hiles, Magd. Coll. Mus. Doc., 1867.
Mus. Bac.—Henry Dawson Sianistreet, Exeter College. Was educated as a chorister at York Cathedral. Proceeded Mus. Doc. at Dublin in 1872, where he died in 1883. He composed several anthems, &c.
Mus. Bac.—Charles Donald Macleane, Exeter Coll. Mus. Doc., 1865.
Mus. Bac.—Charles Garland Verrinder, New Coll. Mus. Doc., Cantuar, 1873.
Mus. Doc.—Charles Frederick Hempel, Magd. Hall. *See* p. 106.

1863.
Mus. Bac.—John Naylor, Magd. Hall. Mus. Doc., 1872.
Mus. Bac.—George Prior, St. Edmund's Hall. Mus. Doc., 1876.

Mus. Bac.—(Rev.) William Henry Bliss, Exeter Coll. B.A., 1862; M.A., 1871.
Mus. Bac.—James Christopher Marks, Magd. Hall. Mus. Doc., 1868.

1864.

Mus. Bac.—William Power O'Donoghue, Magd. Hall.
Mus. Doc.—Richard Haking, Magd. Hall.
Mus. Doc.—Philip Armes, New Coll. *See* p. 106.
Mus. Doc.—Stephen Austen Pearce, New Coll.

1865.

Mus. Bac.—(Rev.) George Purnell Merrick, Exeter Coll. B.A., 1871; M.A., 1878.
Mus. Bac.—Eugene Spinney, Magd. Hall.
Mus. Bac.—Thomas Hewlett, Magd. Hall.
Mus. Bac.—(Rev.) Henry Walter Miller, Corpus Christi Coll., B.A., 1867; M.A., 1875.
Mus. Bac.—William Russell, Christ Church.
Mus. Bac.—Edward Synge, Magd. Hall.
Mus. Doc.—Charles Donald Macleane, Exeter Coll.
Mus. Doc.—John Stainer, Magd. Coll. *See* p. 107.
Mus. Doc.—George French Flowers. *See* p. 103.
Mus. Doc.—James Russell, Magd. Hall.

1866.

Mus. Bac.—(Rev.) Herbert Hall Woodward, Corpus Christi Coll. B.A., 1867; M.A., 1872.
Mus. Bac.—Joseph Crispin Tiley, Magd. Hall. For sixteen years Organist of St. Michael's, Basinghall Street. He proceeded Mus. Doc. from New Coll., 1874. Being possessed of private means he devoted his attention to composition of the highest class, without caring to make money by his work. None of his compositions seem, however, to have been published. He died in 1879, aged 36.
Mus. Bac.—(Rev.) Humphrey Edward Owen, Magd. Hall. B.A. and M.A., 1872.
Mus. Bac.—(Rev.) Reginald Francis Dale, Queen's Coll. B.A., 1866; M.A., 1870.

1867.

Mus. Bac.—George Andus Beaumont Beecroft, Ch. Ch. B.A., 1868; M.A., 1872. Born 1845, his father being M.P. for Leeds. He was an excellent classical and English scholar, a contributor to the *Choir*, a composer, and musical critic. He died in 1873.

Mus. Bac.—William Thomas Belcher, Queen's Coll. Mus. Doc., 1872.

Mus. Bac.—James Hamilton Smee Clarke, Queen's Coll.

Mus. Bac.—H. Baker, New Coll.

Mus. Bac.—(Rev.) Frederick Scotson Clark, Exeter Coll. Born in 1840, Organist of Regent Square Church at the age of fourteen. He was educated at the Royal Academy of Music and at Leipsic. He was Organist successively of several London churches, and afterwards Organist and scholar of Exeter College. In 1867 he became Head Master of a Grammar School at Brighton, after which he entered Holy Orders. In 1878 he obtained a gold medal at the Paris Exhibition as the representative English Organist. He died in 1883. His compositions are all of a popular order, but he was a brilliant extempore player.

Mus. Bac.—Edward Walter Hamilton, C.B., of Ch. Church, afterwards Private Secretary to the Right Hon. W. E. Gladstone.

Mus. Bac.—Charles Hubert Hastings Parry, of Exeter College. B.A., 1870; M.A., 1874; Mus. Doc. by Decree, 1884; Choragus of the University, 1883; Mus. Doc. *honoris causâ* of Cambridge, 1883.

Mus. Doc.—William Pole, F.R.S., St. John's College.

Mus. Doc.—Henry Hiles, Magd. Hall.

Mus. Doc.—Robert Sloman, Christ Church.

1868.

Mus. Bac.—John Frederick Bridge, Queen's Coll. Mus. Doc., 1874.

Mus. Bac.—Francis Everard Willhelm Hulton, New College.

Mus. Bac.—George Clements Martin, New College. Mus. Doc., Cantuar, 1883.

Mus. Bac.—John Barclay Thompson, Queen's Coll. B.A. and Student of Christ Church, 1869; M.A., 1872; Tutor and Proctor, 1878.

Mus. Bac.—John Abram, New Coll. Mus. Doc., 1874.
Mus. Bac.—(Rev.) William Vincent Barnard, New Coll.
Mus. Doc.—James Christopher Marks, Magd. Hall.

1869.

Mus. Bac.—William Thomas Howell Allchin, New Coll. Organist of St. John's, 1875. Died 1883. Composer of a sacred cantata and some songs.
Mus. Bac.—Charles Warwick Jordan, New Coll. Mus. Doc., 1877.
Mus. Bac.—William Creser, New Coll. Mus. Doc., 1880.
Mus. Bac.—Henry Gough Trembath. New Coll.
Mus. Bac.—Haydn Keeton, Magd. Hall. Mus. Doc., 1877.

1870.

D.C.L.—William Sterndale Bennett. *See* p. 143.
Mus. Bac.—Thomas Osborne Marks, New Coll. Mus. Doc., Dublin, 1874.
Mus. Bac.—Albert Lister Peace, New College. Mus. Doc., 1875.
Mus. Bac.—(Rev.) William John Priest, St. Alban's Hall.
Mus. Bac.—William Weaver Ringrose, New Coll.
Mus. Bac.—Roland Rogers, New Coll. Mus. Doc., 1875.
Mus. Bac.—Sydney Hawker Williams, Jesus Coll.
Mus. Bac.—Walter Henry Sangster, New Coll. Mus. Doc., 1877.
Mus. Bac.—Benjamin Agutter, Exeter Coll.
Mus. Bac.—Duncan Thackeray, New Coll. Mus. Doc., Dublin, 1871.

1871.

Mus. Bac.—William Alexander Barrett, St. Mary Hall. Born 1836, was a choirboy at St. Paul's, under Goss, G. Cooper, and Bailey. He was appointed Vicar-Choral of St. Paul's in 1871, the year he took his degree. He died in 1891. He was the editor of the *Orchestra*, *Monthly Musical Record*, and *Musical Times*, and joint-author with Sir John Stainer of the "Dictionary of Musical Terms." He was also eminent as a critic and as a lecturer.*
Mus. Bac.—Charles Harford Lloyd, Magd. Hall. B.A., 1872; M.A. (Hertford Coll.), 1875; Mus. Doc., 1892.

---

* Rudall Carte's "Musical Directory," 1893.

Mus. Bac.—John Varley Roberts, Ch. Ch. Mus. Doc., 1876.
Mus. Bac.—Henry Plumridge, St. Mary Hall. Mus. Doc., 1888.
Mus. Bac.—John Hele, New Coll.
Mus. Bac.—Orlando John Stimpson, New Coll. Incorporated at Durham, 1871.
Mus. Bac.—William Carling, Exeter Coll.
Mus. Bac. —Samuel Reay, New Coll.

1872.
Mus. Bac.—Alfred King, Exeter Coll. Mus. Doc., 1890.
Mus. Bac.—William Samuel Bambridge, Magd. Hall.
Mus. Bac.—(Rev.) Ernest Stuart Bengough, Oriel Coll. B.A., 1861 ; M.A., 1865.
Mus. Bac.—(Rev.) Frederick Peel, Magd. Hall.
Mus. Bac.—Henry Priest, St. Alban Hall.
Mus. Bac.—Joseph Gordon Saunders, Magd. Hall. Mus. Doc. (Hertford Coll.), 1878.
Mus. Doc.—John Naylor, Magd. Hall.
Mus. Doc.—William Thomas Belcher, Queen's Coll.

1873.
Mus. Bac.—Thomas Craddock, New Coll.
Mus. Bac.—Jacob Bradford, New Coll. Mus. Doc., 1878.
Mus. Bac.—Arthur Edwin Dyer, Non-Coll. Mus. Doc., 1880.
Mus. Bac.—Edward William Healey, New Coll.
Mus. Bac.—Frederick Iliffe, New Coll. Mus. Doc., 1879.
Mus. Bac.—Frederick William Pacey, St. Mary Hall.
Mus. Bac.—Walter Parratt, Magd. Coll. Knighted, 1892.
Mus. Bac.—James Taylor, New Coll.
Mus. Bac.—Alexander Walton, St. Mary Hall.

1874.
Mus. Bac.—Charles Bradbury, New Coll.
Mus. Bac.—Hugh Brooksbank, New Coll.
Mus. Bac.—George Herbert Gregory, New Coll.
Mus. Bac.—Charles Hancock, Magd. Hall.
Mus. Bac.—James Higgs, New Coll.
Mus. Bac.—Arthur Henry Mann, New Coll. Mus. Doc., 1882.
Mus. Bac.—Frederick Reynolds Müller, Exeter Coll.
Mus. Bac.—Arthur Simms, New Coll.
Mus. Bac.—George Frederick Tendall, St. Mary Hall.
Mus. Bac.—William Henry Wale, Magd. Hall.

Mus. Bac.—Daniel Joseph Wood, New Coll.
Mus. Bac.—William Pinney, Exeter Coll.
Mus. Doc.—John Abram, New Coll.
Mus. Doc.—John Frederick Bridge, Queen's Coll.
Mus. Doc.—Joseph Crispin Tiley, New Coll. *See* p. 108.

1875.

Mus. Bac.—Edward Henry Birch, New Coll.
Mus. Bac.—Joseph Bradley, New Coll.
Mus. Bac.—George Lawrence Harter Gardner, Ch. Ch. Incorporated from Corpus Christi Coll., Cambridge, in 1873. B.A., 1873; M.A., 1876.
Mus. Bac.—Albert Friedrich Otto Hartmann, Non-Coll.
Mus. Bac.—Arthur Stephen Holloway, Worcester Coll.
Mus. Bac.—Charles Laurence, Hertford Coll.
Mus. Bac.—Thomas Riseley, Ch. Ch.
Mus. Bac.—Brook Sampson, Exeter Coll.
Mus. Bac.—Humphrey John Stark, New Coll.
Mus. Bac.—Thomas Tallis Trimnell, New Coll.
Mus. Bac.—Thomas Troman, New Coll.
Mus. Doc.—Albert Lister Peace, Non-Coll.
Mus. Doc.—Roland Rogers, New Coll.

1876.

Mus. Bac.—John Henry Gower, New Inn Hall. Mus. Doc., 1883.
Mus. Bac.—(Rev.) Henry George Bonavia Hunt, Ch. Ch. Mus. Doc., Dublin, 1887.
Mus. Bac.—(Rev.) Charles Richard Ward, St. John's Coll. B.A., 1874; M.A., 1878.
Mus. Bac.—Robert Henry Wilson, Queen's Coll.
Mus. Bac.—Roland Mellor Winn, New Coll. Mus. Doc., 1883.
Mus. Bac.—Benjamin Bather, New Coll.
Mus. Bac.—Joseph Cox Bridge, Exeter Coll. B.A., 1875; M.A., 1878; Mus. Doc., 1885.
Mus. Bac.—Tom William Dodds, Queen's Coll. Mus. Doc., 1887.
Mus. Bac.—Henry John Edwards, New Coll. Mus. Doc. (Keble), 1885.
Mus. Bac.—Henry Lister, New Coll.
Mus. Bac.—George Lomas, New Coll.
Mus. Bac.—John Browning Lott, New Coll.
Mus. Bac.—Frederick John Read, New Coll. Mus. Doc., 1891.

Mus. Bac.—Ebenezer William Taylor, Hertford Coll. Mus. Doc., 1883.
Mus. Bac.—Charles Lee Williams, New Coll.
Mus. Doc.—John Varley Roberts, Ch. Ch.
Mus. Doc.—George Prior, St. Edmund Hall.

1877.
Mus. Bac.—John Barratt, New Coll.
Mus. Bac.—Richard Allnutt Boissier, Ch. Ch.
Mus. Bac.—Thomas Henry Collinson, New Coll.
Mus. Bac.—Henry Alfred Harding, New Coll. Mus. Doc., 1882.
Mus. Bac.—Henry Walmsley Little, New Coll. Mus. Doc., 1885.
Mus. Bac.—Henry Thomas Pringuer, New Coll. Mus. Doc., 1885.
Mus. Bac.—Frank Joseph Sawyer, New Coll. Mus. Doc., 1884.
Mus. Bac —George Frederick Sims, St. John's Coll.
Mus. Doc.—Haydn Keeton, New Coll.
Mus. Doc.—Walter Henry Sangster, New Coll.

1878.
Mus. Bac.—James Smith Anderson, Queen's Coll.
Mus. Bac.—(Rev.) Arthur Wellesley Batson, St. Alb. Hall.
Mus. Bac.—Edward Brown, New Coll. Mus. Doc., 1883.
Mus. Bac.—Cedric Bucknall, Keble.
Mus. Bac.—Harry Coy, New Coll. Mus. Doc., 1885.
Mus. Bac.—William Henry Garland, New Coll.
Mus. Bac.—John Greig, Queen's Coll. Mus. Doc., 1889.
Mus. Bac.—William Fitzherbert Warner Jackson, New Coll.
Mus. Bac.—Charles Francis Lloyd, New Coll.
Mus. Bac.—Ernest George Meers, Queen's Coll.
Mus. Bac.—Albert George Mitchell, New Coll.
Mus. Bac.—Mark James Monk, New Coll. Mus. Doc., 1888.
Mus. Bac.—Edward Davidson Palmer, New Coll.
Mus. Bac.—James Thomas Pye, New Coll.
Mus. Bac.—George Henry Smith, New Coll.
Mus. Bac.—John Storer, New Coll.
Mus. Bac.—John Frederick Thomason, New Coll.
Mus. Bac.—Henry Stafford Trego, New Coll.
Mus. Bac.—Charles John Vincent, New Coll. Mus. Doc., 1885.
Mus. Bac.—William Robert Wright, New Coll.

Mus. Bac.—James Grindrod Wrigley, New Coll.
Mus. Doc.—Jacob Bradford, New Coll.
Mus. Doc.—Joseph Gordon Saunders, Hertford Coll.

1879.

Mus. Bac.—William Bennis Alcock, New Coll.
Mus. Bac.—Edward Johnson Bellerby, New Coll.
Mus. Bac.—Frederick Bentley, New Coll.
Mus. Bac.—Francis Drake Carnell, New Coll.
Mus. Bac.—Thomas Hutchinson, New Coll.
Mus. Bac.—Arthur William Marchant, New Coll.
Mus. Bac.—Thomas Palmer, New Coll.
Mus. Bac.—Charles Seal, New Coll.
Mus. Bac.—Joseph Watson Sidebotham, New Coll.
Mus. Bac.—George Henry Stone, New Coll.
Mus. Doc.—Frederick Iliffe, New Coll.

Honorary Degrees.

Mus. Doc.—George Alexander Macfarren, Trin. Coll., Cambridge. See p. 146.
Mus. Doc.—Sir Herbert Stanley Oakeley, Ch. Ch. B.A., 1853; M.A., 1856; Mus. Doc., Cambridge, 1871; LL.D., Aberdeen, 1881; D.C.L., Toronto, 1886; Mus. Doc., Dublin, 1887; Professor of Music at Edinburgh University, 1865 to 1891; Knighted, 1876.
Mus. Doc.—Arthur Seymour Sullivan, Trin. Coll., Cambridge. See p. 147.

These are the first Honorary Degrees in Music conferred by the University of Oxford.

1880.

Mus. Bac.—Frederick William Clarke, Queen's Coll. Died 1883, aged thirty-one.
Mus. Bac.—John Maude Crament, Non-Coll.
Mus. Bac.—Basil Harwood, Trinity Coll. B.A., 1881; M.A., 1884.
Mus. Bac.—Theodore Stephen Tearne, New Coll.
Mus. Bac.—Henry Walter, Charsley Hall.
Mus. Doc.—Arthur Edwin Dyer, Non-Coll.
Mus. Doc.—William Creser, New Coll.

1881.
Mus. Bac.—Hubert Lamb, New Coll.
Mus. Bac.—Edward Mills, New Coll.
Mus. Bac.—Samuel Myerscough, Hertf. Coll.

1882.
Mus. Bac.—George Cockle, Exeter Coll. B.A., Trin. Coll., Camb., 1851; M.A., 1854.
Mus. Bac.—(Rev.) John Henry Mee, Queen's Coll. B.A. and Fellow of Merton, 1875; M.A., 1878; Mus. Doc., 1888; Coryphæus, 1891.
Mus. Bac.—William Claxton, Trinity Coll. B.A., 1876.
Mus. Bac.—Arthur Blurton Plant, New Coll.
Mus. Doc.—Arthur Henry Mann, New Coll.
Mus. Doc.—Henry Alfred Harding, New Coll.

1883.
Mus. Bac.—George Emery, New Coll.
Mus. Bac.—(Rev.) Arthur Henry Stevens, Keble Coll. B.A., 1881; M.A., 1884.
Mus. Bac.—William Alfred Wrigley, New Coll.
Mus. Bac.—John Hayman Righton, New Coll.
Mus. Bac.—William Good Merrikin, New Coll.
Mus. Bac.—Frederick Robert Greenish, New Coll. Mus. Doc., 1891.
Mus. Doc.—Edward Brown, New Coll.
Mus. Doc.—John Henry Gower, New Inn Hall.
Mus. Doc.—Ebenezer William Taylor, New Coll.
Mus. Doc.—Roland Mellor Winn, New Coll.

Honorary Degree.
Mus. Doc.—Charles Villiers Stanford, M.A., Trin. Coll., Cambridge.

1884.
Mus. Bac.—Leonard James Rogers, Balliol Coll. B.A., 1884; M.A., 1887.
Mus. Bac.—Frank Osmond Carr, New Coll. Mus. Doc., 1891. *See* p. 149.
Mus. Bac.—James Langran, Hertford.
Mus. Doc.—Charles Hubert Hastings Parry, Exeter Coll. Created by decree of Convocation.
Mus. Doc.—Frank Joseph Sawyer.

1885.

Mus. Bac.—William Alexander Campbell Cruickshank, Keble Coll.
Mus. Bac.—Theophilus Hemmings, New Coll.
Mus. Bac.—Reginald Bowerman Moore, New Coll.
Mus. Bac.—Frederick Pugh, New Coll.
Mus. Doc.—Joseph Cox Bridge, Exeter Coll.
Mus. Doc.—Harry Coy, New Coll.
Mus. Doc.—Henry John Edwards, Keble Coll.
Mus. Doc.—Henry Walmsley Little, New Coll.
Mus. Doc.—Henry Thomas Pringuer, New Coll.
Mus. Doc.—Charles John Vincent, New Coll.

HONORARY DEGREE.
Mus. Doc.—Hans Richter.

1886.
Mus. Bac.—William George Price, Queen's Coll.
Mus. Bac.—Franz Koeller, New Coll.
Mus. Bac.—Herbert Theodore Lewis, Ch. Ch.
Mus. Bac.—Frederick James Simpson, New Coll.
Mus. Bac.—Daniel Ferguson Wilson, New Coll.

1887.
Mus. Bac.—Joseph Summers, New Coll.
Mus. Bac.—William Wolstenholme, Worcester Coll.
Mus. Bac.—Robert Bowness Bateman, New Coll.
Mus. Bac.—Joseph Matthias Field, New Coll.
Mus. Bac.—Charles John Revell, New Coll.
Mus. Bac.—Thomas Henry Yorke Trotter, New Coll. B.A., 1878; M.A., 1887; Mus. Doc., 1892.
Mus. Doc.—Tom William Dodds, Queen's Coll.

1888.
Mus. Bac.—Charles Edward Jolley, New Coll.
Mus. Bac.—(Rev.) Septimus Ernest Luke Spooner Lillingston, Hertford Coll. B.A., 1886; M.A., 1889.
Mus. Bac.—Samuel Symons Martyn, Keble Coll.
Mus. Bac.—Henry Ernest Nichol, New Coll.
Mus. Bac.—Alfred Madeley Richardson, Keble Coll. B.A., 1888; M.A., 1892.

Mus. Bac.—William Edmund Stevenson, New Coll.
Mus. Bac.—William Edwin Thomas, St. Edm. H.
Mus. Doc.—Mark James Monk, New Coll.
Mus. Doc.—Walter Bond Gilbert, New Coll.
Mus. Doc.—(Rev.) John Henry Mee, Merton Coll. See p. 115.
Mus. Doc.—Henry Plumridge, Keble Coll.

1889.
Mus. Bac.—Joseph Humfrey Anger, New Coll.
Mus. Bac.—Henry Coward, Queen's Coll.
Mus. Bac.—Alfred Stanley Dale, Brasenose Coll.
Mus. Bac.—Clement Rowland Gale, Exeter Coll. B.A., 1886.
Mus. Bac.—Matthew Henry Peacock, Exeter Coll. B.A., 1880; M.A., 1883.
Mus. Bac.—Edward Thomas Sweeting, New Coll.
Mus. Bac.—Amhurst Webber, New Coll.
Mus. Bac.—Charles Francis Abdy Williams, Ch. Ch.
Mus. Doc.—John Greig, Queen's Coll.

1890.
Mus. Bac.—Frank Nicholson Abernethy, New Coll.
Mus. Bac.—William Agate, Queen's Coll.
Mus. Bac.—Edred Martin Chaundy, Non-Coll. B.A., 1890.
Mus. Bac.—William George Eveleigh, Queen's Coll.
Mus. Bac.—William Henry Hadow, Worcester Coll. B.A., 1882; M.A., 1885; Fellow of Worcester, 1888.
Mus. Bac.—Raoul de Dreux Kunz, New Coll.
Mus. Bac.—Charles Tom Reynolds, New Coll.
Mus. Bac.—William Arthur Baker Russell, New Coll.
Mus. Bac.—Thomas Smith, Queen's Coll.
Mus. Bac.—Frederick Stamps, Queen's Coll.
Mus. Bac.—(Rev.) Walter Grenville Whinfield, Magd. Coll. B.A., 1889.
Mus. Doc.—Alfred King, Exeter Coll.

1891.
Mus. Bac.—John Edmund Barkworth, Univ. Coll. B.A., 1881; M.A., 1884.
Mus. Bac.—Daniel Bradfield, New Coll.
Mus. Bac.—Arthur Charles Edwards, St. Edm. H.

Mus. Bac.—Albert Jowett, Queen's Coll.
Mus. Bac.—Clement Charlton Palmer, Non-Coll.
Mus. Bac.—(Rev.) Geoffrey Charles Edward Ryley, Trinity Coll. B.A., 1889.
Mus. Bac.—Ferris Tozer, Queen's Coll.
Mus. Bac.—Albert Williams, New Coll.
Mus. Bac.—Archibald Wayet Wilson, Keble Coll.
Mus. Bac.—Francis Cunningham Woods, Exeter Coll. B.A., 1889 ; M.A., 1890.
Mus. Doc.—Frederick Robert Greenish, New Coll.
Mus. Doc.—Charles Harford Lloyd, Ch. Ch. *See* p. 110.
Mus. Doc.—Frank Osmond Carr, New Coll.
Mus. Doc.—Frederick John Read, New Coll.

1892.

Mus. Bac.—Percy Charles Buck, Worcester Coll.
Mus. Bac.—Franklin Sievewright Peterson, New Coll.
Mus. Bac.—Ivor Algernon Atkins, Queen's Coll.
Mus. Bac.—Thomas Popplewell Royle, Magd. Coll. B.A., 1889; M.A., 1892.
Mus. Bac.—(Rev.) Frederick William Bussell, Brasenose Coll. B.A., 1885 ; M.A., 1888 ; B.D., 1893 ; Fellow of Brasenose Coll., 1886.
Mus. Bac.—William Willoughby, Non-Coll.
Mus. Doc.—Thomas Henry Yorke Trotter, New Coll.

1893.

Mus. Bac.—Ernest Walker, B.A., Balliol College.
Mus. Bac.—FitzWilliam de Gaudaloupe English, M.A., St. Mary Hall.
Mus. Bac.—Montague Frederick Alderson, B.A., Merton Coll.
Mus. Bac.—Norman Burrell Hibbert, Queen's Coll.
Mus. Bac.—Arnold Kennedy, Queen's Coll.
Mus. Bac.—Frank Hodson Cliffe, B.A., St. Mary Hall.
Mus. Bac.—Hugh P. Allen, Queen's Coll.
Mus. Doc.—William Edwin Thomas, St. Edmund Hall.

CHAPTER X.

CAMBRIDGE GRADUATES IN MUSIC.

1463.

Mus. Bac.—Henry Habyngton, Abyngton, or Abyngdon, was admitted February 20, and was allowed to proceed to the degree of Doctor in Music on condition of his remaining one year in Cambridge after receiving the Baccalauriat.* Why this condition was imposed is not clear, unless it was that the University wished to retain for a period the services of so eminent a musician. Whether he fulfilled the condition is not stated. He was a friend of Sir Thomas More, who wrote two Latin epitaphs on him (in Cayley's "Life of More," I., 317). He is called in these "Nobilis," as was a contemporary, John Atkins, Fellow of Merton, who is styled in the album of that house "Nobilis Musicus." † He was appointed Succentor of Wells Cathedral in 1447, Master of the Song of the Chapel Royal in 1465, at a salary of forty marks, and Master of St. Catherine's Hospital, Bristol, in 1478. The following extract from one of More's epitaphs shows that he was of great reputation as a singer and organist :

Millibus in mille cantor fuit optimus ille,
Præter et hæc ista fuit optimus orgaquenista :

He died in 1497, and was succeeded in his post at Wells (which he held together with his other appointments) by Robert Wydow.

Mus. Doc.—Thomas Saintwix, Saintvist, or Saint Just, who had previously received the degree of Doctor in Music, was this year made Master of King's Hall ‡ by Edward IV., whose Chaplain he was.§ He died in 1467.

---

* Appendix, B. C.   † Wood, "Annals," II., Bk. II., 722.
‡ King's Hall was afterwards, with Michael House and Bishop's and Garrett's Hostels, merged into Trinity College. Burney and Hawkins confuse it with King's College, with which it had no connection.   § App. D.

1470.

Mus. Bac.—Lessy, a member of the Duke of York's Chapel.*

1489.

Mus. Bac.—According to Baker, one person received this degree, but his name is not known.

1496.

Mus. Bac.—Humfrey Fryvill, or Frevill, who had studied at Cambridge for two years, and elsewhere for five.† He proceeded Mus. Doc. in 1504. Nothing is known of his life.

1497.

Mus. Bac.— —— Pypis.

1501—2.

Mus. Doc.—Robert Fayrfax,‡ Fairfax or Ferfax, of an ancient Yorkshire family. He was born probably about 1470. He was Organist of St. Alban's Abbey, which at that time contained the finest organ in England, built in 1438. In 1511 he incorporated at Oxford, and the composition which he performed on that occasion, consisting of a Gloria in five parts, is preserved in a fine choir book at Lambeth Palace. About 1509 he was appointed one of the Gentlemen of the King's Chapel. In 1514 he was allowed 12d. a day as one of the poor Knights of Windsor. He added considerably to his income by making copies of choir books, of which the celebrated MS. mentioned by Burney and Hawkins is probably one. He died in 1529-30, and was buried at St. Alban's. Portions of his compositions are in the University Library at Cambridge, at St. John's and Caius Colleges, in the Music School at Oxford, and the Fayrfax MS. in the British Museum (Add. MSS., 5,465 and 31,922). Hawkins, p. 356, gives a three-part Motet, "Ave summe æternitatis," by him, and Burney, "That was my woo,"§ two movements from his Mass "Albanus,"‖ and a Gloria¶ from another Mass, all for three voices. A madrigal, "I love, loved, and loved would be," by him, was published in 1891 by the Plainsong and Mediæval Music Society.

---

* App. E.   † App. F.   ‡ App. G.   § Vol. II., p. 546.
‖ *Ibid.*, pp. 561 and 563.   ¶ *Ibid.*, p. 564.

1502.

Mus. Bac.—John Parker, who studied for three and a half years at Cambridge.

Mus. Bac.—Robert Wydow, Wydewe, or Wedow, incorporated from Oxford,* where he was educated, and where he distinguished himself in poetry and music, and took the degree of Bachelor in Music. In 1481 he was presented, by Edward IV., to the living of Thaxted, in Essex, his birthplace. This he resigned in 1489, and travelled in France and Italy, where he gained the appellation of "Grammaticus." In 1497 he succeeded Habyngton as Succentor of Wells Cathedral. About 1499 he was made deputy for the transaction of affairs between the Pope and the Chapter of Wells Cathedral. His benefactions to the Carthusian Priory of Henton, near Bath, were so large, that a Requiem was sung for his soul in every house of the order in England. He died in 1505. Holinshed classes him among the celebrities of Henry VII.'s reign. For further particulars of his life, see Grove's Dictionary, Vol. IV., p. 817.

1504.

Mus. Doc.—Humfrey Fryvill. *See* p. 120.

Mus. Doc.—Robert Cooper, Coper or Cowper, a priest,† who was already a Bachelor of Music. He is mentioned in Morley's Catalogue of Famous Musicians. There is a song by him, "Petyously constrayned am I," in the British Museum (Royal MSS., App. No. 58), and another, "Alone I live," was published by the Plainsong and Mediæval Music Society in 1891.

1507.

Mus. Bac.—Robert Porret, or Perrot.‡ He graduated as Mus. Doc. at Oxford in 1515. *See* p. 66.

1516.

Mus. Bac.—John Watkins, a priest, who had studied music seven years.§

---

* App. G. † App. H. ‡ Baker MSS., Vol. XXIV., p. 12. § App. I.

Mus. Bac.—John Firtun, a priest, one of the Vicars of St. Stephen's, Westminster, and a member of Lord Norfolk's Chapel. He was required to compose a Mass and an Antiphon.*

1517.

Mus. Bac.—Thomas Burrow, or Borow.

Mus. Bac.— —— Plummer, a priest.

1519.

Mus. Bac.—Benjamin Beryderyke, a teacher of music, who had studied the "speculation of music" one year at Cambridge, and five years elsewhere. He was required to compose a Mass before taking his degree.†

1534.

Mus. Bac.—Henry Crosse, a priest.

1536.

Mus. Bac.—Christopher Tye, who had studied, and taught music to boys, for ten years.‡ He was, in Burney's opinion, as great a musician as Europe could then boast. He was born at Westminster, and became first a Chorister, then a Gentleman of the Chapel Royal. He proceeded Doctor in Music in 1545.§ During the reign of Henry VIII. he was distinguished for his setting of Masses and Motets to Latin words. Burney gives a portion of his fine Mass "Euge bone."|| Baker tells us that he instructed Edward VI. in music; and he afterwards became Organist to Queen Elizabeth's Chapel. On what terms he was with the latter sovereign may be judged from the following anecdote quoted by Hawkins ¶ from the Ashmolean MSS. : "Dr. Tye was a peevish and humoursome man, especially in his latter days; and sometimes playing on the organ in the Chapel of Queen Elizabeth, which contained much music, but little delight to the ear, she would send the Verger to tell him that he played out of tune; whereupon he sent word that her ears were out of tune." When the Church Service had to be rendered in English, Tye translated the first fourteen chapters of the

---

* App. J.   † App. K.   ‡ App. L.   § App. M.
|| Vol. II., p. 589.   ¶ Page 455.

Acts of the Apostles into English metre, and set them to music; but they were not a success, for Tye, though he had a good reputation as a literary man, was no poet. Hawkins* quotes a portion of this work, consisting of a fine Canon to words beginning "It chanced in Iconium, as we ofttimes did use." After this he set selections from the Psalms, which compositions he called anthems, a corruption of antiphon. In 1541 he became Organist of Ely Cathedral, and held this post till 1561, when he was probably appointed to the Royal Chapel. In 1548 he incorporated at Oxford. He died about 1580. Compositions by him are preserved in the Music School and at Ch. Ch., Oxford, in the Tudway collection, in Rimbault's and Boyce's Cathedral Music, in Barnard's Church Music, in Page's "Harmonia Sacra," and in Mulliner's MS. (Add. MSS., 30,513). He was in Holy Orders, and held successively the Rectories of Little Wilbraham, Newton, and Doddington-cum-March, all in Cambridgeshire. Tye was the first of the great school of composers for the English Cathedral Service, and prepared the ground for Tallis and Bird. Wood attributes to him the restoration of Church music, after it had been ruined by the dissolution of the monasteries.

1545.
Mus. Doc.—Christopher Tye. *See* p. 122.

1561.
Mus. Bac.—Robert White, Wight † or Whytt. He is mentioned by Morley in his Introduction, and is ranked by him with Orlando Lasso, and as one of the famous Englishmen who have been nothing inferior to the best composers on the Continent. About 1562 he succeeded Tye as Magister Choristarum of Ely, at a salary of £10 per annum; and previously to this he had apparently been Organist of Westminster Abbey. Few particulars of his life seem known, and only a few of his compositions have been printed.‡ There

---

* Page 454.
† In the grace granting him his degree his name is spelt thus. See App. N.
‡ One by Burney, Vol. III., p. 67.

are some in MS. in Ch. Ch. Library. An entry recently found in the marriage register of Trinity Church, Ely, leads to the supposition that White was Christopher Tye's son-in-law. He died in 1574, and his will describes him as Master of the Choristers of Westminster Abbey. In a set of his Latin Anthems and Services at Ch. Ch. the following distich occurs :—

> Maxima Musarum nostrarum gloria White
> Tu peris; æternum sed tua musa manet.*

1577.

Mus. Bac.—Richard Carleton, Charlton or Carlton. He was educated at Clare Hall, and proceeded B.A. this year, and Mus. Bac. shortly afterwards. He was in priest's orders, and held some appointment at Norwich Cathedral. He was the composer of a collection of twenty-one madrigals in 1601, and a contributor to the "Triumphs of Oriana." In 1612 he was given the living of Bawsey and Glosthorp, near Lynn, and probably died in 1638.

1586.

Mus. Bac.—William Blitheman, Master of the Choristers of Ch. Ch., Oxford, in 1564, and one of the Organists of the Chapel Royal. Hawkins gives an organ piece by him,† and there are compositions in Queen Elizabeth's Virginal Book, and in the Mulliner MS. in the British Museum (Add. MSS., 30,513). He was the Instructor of John Bull, according to the brass plate which was over his tomb in St. Nicholas Olave, Queenhithe. He died in 1591.

1594.

Mus. Bac.—Edward Johnson, of Caius Coll. Composer of a madrigal in Morley's "Triumphs of Oriana," 1601, and some Psalm tunes in Est's "Whole Book of Psalms," 1592. Some MS. madrigals by him are in the Library of the Royal College of Music, and in the British Museum (Add. MSS., 30,484).

1601.

Mus. Bac.—One person took this degree, but no name is given.

---

* Burney, Vol. III., p. 66, note.   † P. 931.

1605.

Mus. Bac.—Thomas Bangcrofte.

1606.

Mus. Bac.—Orlando Gibbons,* born at Cambridge in 1583, son of William Gibbons, one of the Waits† of Cambridge. He became a chorister in King's in 1596, under his brother Edward. In 1604 he succeeded Arthur Cock as Organist of the Chapel Royal. In 1611 he contributed several masterly works to "Parthenia." In 1612 he published a first set of madrigals and motets "apt for viols and voices." Other compositions by him are in "Benjamin Cosyn's Virginal Book" at Buckingham Palace, "Queen Elizabeth's Virginal Book" at the Fitzwilliam Museum, and in the British Museum (Add. MSS., 29,996 and 31,403). He was one of the first to write for stringed instruments, as distinguished from pieces intended equally for voices or strings. His "Fantasies of Three Parts," about 1622, were the first compositions engraved on copper plates. In Add. MSS., 39,372-7, and in the library of the Royal College of Music, there is a burlesque madrigal by him, "The Cries of London." He wrote a large amount of Church music, the whole of which was edited by the Rev. Sir F. Ouseley in 1873. In 1614 he contributed some hymns to Sir W. Leighton's "Teares and Lamentacions," and to G. Withers' Hymns and Songs of the Church. In 1622, Gibbons accumulated the degrees of Bachelor and Doctor of Music at Oxford, the University having been requested by Camden to confer these degrees on him and William Heather. It seems probable that he wrote Heather's Exercise for him (*see* p. 78). In 1625 Charles I. commissioned Gibbons to compose and conduct the music for the reception of Henrietta Maria at Canterbury, in carrying out which commission he was seized with an apoplectic fit, and died on

---

* App. O.
† The Waits were watchmen who played on Hautboys (called also Wayts) at the hours during the night. More than one eminent musician began life in this way (John Ravenscroft, died 1745; Farmer, Mus. Bac., *see* p. 130). They took an important place in the household of Edward IV., where they ranked with the Minstrels.

5th of June, and was buried in Canterbury Cathedral. He was one of the most famous of our native composers, and has been called the "Palestrina of England."*

Mus. Bac.—Michael East, Easte, Est, or Este.† His publications, which are more numerous than those of any of his contemporaries, consist of madrigals, anthems, and other works He contributed, in 1601, to the "Triumphs of Oriana." Williams, Bishop of Lincoln, settled an annuity on him in return for the pleasure he had received from hearing some of East's motets. Little is known of his life. He was probably the son of Thomas East, the music printer. About 1618 he became Master of the Choristers at Lichfield Cathedral. It is not known when he died, but his last composition, a set of duos and fancies for the viol, was published in 1638.

1607.

Mus. Bac.—Thomas Ravenscroft. Born about 1582. Educated under Pearce as a chorister at St. Paul's Cathedral. Little seems known of his life or of when he died. He published the first collection of canons and rounds printed in this country, entitled "Pammelia," in 1609. Other of his publications were "Deuteromelia" (later in 1609), a second part of "Pammelia," "Melismata," a collection of Phansies for three, four, and five voices, in 1614; a work on Musical Mensuration in 1611; "The whole Booke of Psalmes; with the Hymnes Evangelicall and Spirituall," in 1621; and there are four MS. anthems by him at Ch. Ch., Oxford.

1608.

Mus. Bac.—John Tomkins,‡ son of Rev. Thomas Tomkins, Minor Canon of Gloucester. He was born in 1586, and became Organist of King's College, Cambridge, in 1606. He belonged to a large family of musicians, and was a brother of Thomas Tomkins, Mus. Bac., of Oxford (see page 76). Later in life he became Organist of St. Paul's Cathedral and a member of the Chapel Royal, and died in 1638. Barnard's collection contains some anthems by him.

---

* By Fétis, "Biog. gen. des Musiciens."
† Baker MSS., Vol. XXIV., p. 296.
‡ Baker MSS., Vol. XXIV., p. 296. See App. P.

1610.
Mus. Bac.—James Wever.
Mus. Bac.—George Brett.

1616.
Mus. Bac.—Robert Ramsey, who had studied seven years. He was required to compose a "Canticum" to be performed at St. Mary's Church at the Comitia, and he was allowed to be presented for his degree in the dress of a Bachelor of Arts.* In the Tudway Collection there is a Service in F by "Mr. Ramsey, Organist of Trinity College in Cambridge, 1639." No christian name is given, though a space is left for it by Tudway, in the index. The general catalogue of the MS. music in the British Museum, published in 1842, following Burney in his catalogue of the Tudway MSS., gives the name of the author of the above service as John Ramsey, but there is nothing to show that this "Mr." Ramsey is not the Robert Ramsey who took his degree in 1616. Some of his anthems are at Ely and Peterhouse, Cambridge.

Mus. Bac.—One other person, whose name is unknown, took this degree.

1617.
Mus. Bac.—One person. Name unknown.

1626.
Mus. Bac.—John Hilton, of Trinity College, who also proceeded M.A. in the same year. In 1628 he became Organist of St. Margaret's, Westminster, and Clerk of the Parish. His first publication probably was his contribution to the "Triumphs of Oriana," in 1601. In 1627 he published a book of Fa las for three voices, and in 1652 a collection of Rounds and Catches by himself and other composers, called "Catch who catch can." Several of his madrigals have been republished of late years, and some of his Church music is in Rimbault's Cathedral music. There are some MS. compositions by him in the British Museum. Burney gives his canon "Non nobis Domine" (Vol. III., p. 416). He died in 1657, and was buried at St. Margaret's, Westminster.

---

* App. Q.

1640.

Mus. Bac.—Henry Loosemore, Organist of King's College, Cambridge, and, in 1660, of Exeter Cathedral. Compositions by him are in the Tudway Collection, at Ely, at Peterhouse, and in Jebb's " Choral Responses and Litanies." He died in 1670.

Mus. Bac.—John Amner, incorporated from Oxford. *See* p. 78.

1651.

Mus. Doc.—Charles Coleman, or Colman, previously a member of Charles I.'s private band. He had settled in London during the Rebellion as a private teacher of music, and was recommended for the degree of Mus. Doc. by the committee appointed for the reformation of the University in 1651. He takes an important place in history as one of those who contributed music to the first English Opera, the "Siege of Rhodes," by Davenant, produced at Rutland House in 1656. Previously to this the English language had been considered incapable of being used for recitative. His co-operators were Henry Lawes, Captain Cooke, and Mathew Locke. After the Restoration, Coleman and his son became violists in the royal band; and in 1662 he was appointed composer to the King in succession to Henry Lawes. He died in 1664. Many collections contain music by him, and there are MSS. in the Fitzwilliam Museum, Lambeth Palace, the British Museum, and Christ Church, Oxford.

1658.

Mus. Bac.—Benjamin Rogers, born in 1614, was chorister and lay clerk at St. George's, Windsor. He became Organist at Christ Church, Dublin, but was obliged to leave because of the Rebellion; he then became again lay clerk of St. George's, but was dismissed in 1644, on the breaking up of the choir. After this he supported himself by teaching music in Windsor. He composed, in 1653, some music for organ and violin, which was performed before Archduke Leopold, afterwards Emperor of Germany, and which made a favourable impression on him. On the Restoration he became Organist of Eton College, and, shortly after, lay clerk of St. George's. He was appointed Informator Choristarum of Magd. College, Oxford, in 1664, and proceeded Doctor in Music at that University in 1669. He died in 1698. He was the composer of much Church music, some of which is in the collections of Boyce, Rimbault, and Sir F. Ouseley, and much is in MS. in various cathedrals and college chapels. He was also the composer of some Glees, and the well-known grace "*Te Deum Patrem colimus*," which is sung daily at Magd. College, and annually on May 1, on the tower, in the early morning.

1665.

Mus. Doc.—George Loosemore, Organist, in 1660, of Trinity College, son of Henry, and brother of John, the organ builder. There are some anthems by him in the Tudway Collection and at Ely Cathedral.

1671.

Mus. Doc.—John Ferrabosco, by royal letters of James II. He was Organist of Ely, where some of his anthems are preserved. He died in 1682. He is supposed to have been the grandson of Alphonso Ferrabosco the elder, an Italian composer who settled in England during Elizabeth's reign.

1681.

Mus. Bac.—Thomas Tudway. Born about 1650. In 1670 he succeeded Henry Loosemore as Organist of King's College, Cambridge, and afterwards held the organistship of Pembroke in addition. On January 30, 1704-5, he succeeded Staggins as Professor of Music. In 1705 his anthem "Thou, O God, hast heard our desire," was performed before Queen Anne in King's College, as the exercise for his degree of Mus. Doc., and he was given the title of Composer and Organist extraordinary to the Queen. On July 28, 1706, Tudway was cited before the Vice-Chancellor for having spoken words highly reflecting on the Queen, and an Act in the public register runs as follows: "That Mr. Tudway be suspended from all degrees, taken and to be taken; that he be deprived of his organist's place in St. Mary's Church, and of his Professorship of Music in the University."* He was also deprived of

---

* Cooper. "Annals of Cambridge," Vol. IV., p. 77.

the organistship at King's and Pembroke, but was reinstated in all his posts the following year. Part of his offence was that, being an inveterate punster, he remarked, *apropos* of the Chancellor, the Duke of Somerset, who caused dissatisfaction at the paucity of his patronage: " The Chancellor rides us all, without a bit in our mouths." In 1726 he resigned his College appointments, and was employed by Lord Harley in forming the well-known collection of compositions by English musicians, now in the British Museum (Harleian MSS., 7,337-7,342). Several of his own compositions are included in this collection, the catalogue of which is given in Grove's Dictionary, Vol. IV., page 198. He died in 1730.

1682.

Mus. Doc.—Nicholas Staggins, by letters patent. He was a pupil of his father, a musician of no great attainments, and was appointed in 1682 Master of Charles II.'s band of music, through royal favour, since he had no particular abilities. To him is due the foundation of the Professorship of Music at Cambridge, which title was conferred on him in 1684 under the circumstances mentioned in Chapter V. He composed Odes for the birthdays of William III. and Anne, some songs in "Choice Ayres, Songs, and Dialogues," 1673, and some music for Dryden's " Conquest of Granada," part of which is in Smith's *Musica antiqua*. He died in 1705.

1684.

Mus. Bac.—John Abell, probably the celebrated lutenist and alto singer, who was born about 1660, and was sworn a Gentleman of the Chapel Royal on May 1, 1679. He went to Italy to cultivate his voice, and returned in 1681-2. He was dismissed from the Chapel Royal in 1688 as a Papist, and went abroad. In 1698 he became Intendant at Cassel. He returned to England about 1700, and is said to have been at Cambridge in his later years. The date of his death is unknown.

Mus. Bac.—Thomas Farmer, originally a " Wait " in London (*see* note, p. 125). He composed some vocal and instrumental music for the theatre, some songs, and two " Consorts of Musick" in four parts. He also contributed to Playford's " Choice Ayres " in 1675. He died about 1695, and Purcell composed an elegy on him, which is included in "Orpheus Britannicus."

1696.

Mus. Bac.—Robert King, of St. Catherine's Hall, a member of the band of William and Mary and Queen Anne. He was a prolific composer of songs, and also wrote music to Shadwell's Ode on St. Cecilia's Day, and Peter Molleux's Ode on John Cecil, Earl of Exeter. Nothing is known of his life.

Mus. Bac.—Moses Snow, of St. Catherine's Hall, a Gentleman of the Chapel Royal and Lay Vicar of Westminster Abbey. He died in 1702. He was the father of Valentine Snow, for whom Handel wrote the trumpet parts in his oratorios.

Mus. Doc.—William Turner. Born in 1651, was a chorister under Edward Lowe, of Christ Church, Oxford, and afterwards under Captain Cook at the Chapel Royal. He was part-composer with John Blow and Pelham Humfrey of the "Club Anthem." He became a tenor singer at Lincoln Cathedral, and in 1669 a Gentleman of the Chapel Royal, afterwards a Vicar-Choral of St. Paul's, and Lay Vicar of Westminster Abbey. He composed much church music, some of which is in the Tudway Collection, Ely Cathedral, and the choir-books of the Chapel Royal and Westminster Abbey. Many of his songs were printed in various collections of his time. He died in 1739-40, aged eighty-eight.

1698.

Mus. Bac.—Francis Piggott. Was elected Organist of Magdalen College, Oxford, in 1687, and First Organist of the Temple Church in 1688. Organist Extraordinary of the Chapel Royal in 1695, and Organist in Ordinary on the death of Child in 1697. He composed some anthems. He died in 1704.

Mus. Bac.—Charles Quarles, Organist of Trinity College. In 1722 he became Organist of York Minster. He died in 1727. The only composition by him known is "A Lesson for the Harpsichord," printed by Goodison about 1788.

Mus. Bac.—Thomas Wanless, Organist of York Minster. The "York Litany" by him (printed in Jebbs' Responses) has many versions, and it is supposed that no two copies agree. There is an anthem by him in the Tudway Collection. He died in 1721.

1705.

Mus. Doc.—Thomas Tudway. *See* p. 129.

1710.

Mus. Bac.—Shelton Beeston.

1719.

Mus. Bac.—James Hawkins. Was a Chorister at St. John s Coll., and Organist of Ely from 1682 to his death in 1729. Seventy-five anthems and seventeen services by him are at Ely in MS., and several others in the Tudway Collection.

Mus. Bac.—Rouse Hawley.
Mus. Bac.—William Weale.

1720.

Mus. Bac.—Thomas Woodroffe.

1724.

Mus. Bac.—Robert Fuller, of King's College.

1725.

Mus. Bac.—John Bennett.

1730.

Mus. Doc.—Maurice Greene. Born about 1696, was a Chorister at St. Paul's under Charles King, and was afterwards articled to Brind, Organist of the Cathedral. In 1716 he was appointed Organist of St. Dunstan's in the West, Fleet Street, and in 1717 succeeded Daniel Purcell as Organist of St. Andrew's, Holborn. In 1718 he became Organist of St. Paul's, in succession to Brind, and in 1727 succeeded Croft, as Organist and Composer to the Chapel Royal. At one time he was on friendly terms with Handel, whom he admitted to play on the organ at St. Paul's; but the friendship cooled when Handel discovered that he was on equally good terms with Bononcini. In 1728, Greene, having withdrawn from the "Academy of Ancient Music," owing to the dismissal of Bononcini,* established, in con-

---

* The reason for Bononcini's dismissal was that he was suspected of having passed off a composition by Lotti as his own.

junction with Festing, a rival concert, called "The Apollo," near Temple Bar. The meetings took place in the Devil Tavern, and Handel is said to have remarked that "Toctor Greene had gone to the Devil." In 1730 he succeeded Tudway as Professor of Music at Cambridge, and was made a Doctor of Music. His exercise was Pope's "Ode on St. Cecilia's Day," altered, and adapted to the occasion of the opening of the newly built Senate House. Hawkins gives a quotation from it on page 880. He also, on the same occasion, performed two new anthems at St. Mary's Church.* In 1735 Greene succeeded Eccles as Master of George II.'s band. In 1750 he was left an estate in Essex worth £700 a year, by his uncle, Serjeant Greene. He then began to form a collection of the best English Cathedral Music, the materials of which he left to his friend, Dr. Boyce, on his death in 1755. Besides his exercise, his compositions consist of many Odes for the King's Birthday and New Year's Day. Forty select anthems (1743), a Te Deum with orchestral accompaniment, numerous anthems, two oratorios, several pastoral operas and masques, many songs, some catches and canons, and some organ and harpsichord music. He was one of the founders of the Society of Musicians. In 1888 his body was moved from St. Olave's, Jewry, and re-interred in St. Paul's Cathedral. Although Greene was a most skilful contrapuntist, and is the only Englishman ranked by Matheson among the eminent organists of Europe, he introduced the baneful practice of playing "solos" on particular stops, with an accompaniment on a different manual, in order to please an uneducated audience.†

1744.

Mus. Bac.—John Randall. Born in 1715; was a Chorister of the Chapel Royal, under Bernard Gates. He was appointed about 1745 Organist of King's College, and in 1755 succeeded Greene as Professor of Music. He proceeded Mus. Doc. in 1756, and in 1768 composed the music for the installation of the Duke of Grafton as Chancellor of the University. He died in 1799. He composed some Church music and two double chants.

---

* Cooper, "Annals of Cambridge," Vol. IV., p. 208.   † Hawkins. 884.

1748.

Mus. Bac.—John Worgan. Born in 1724; was a pupil of his brother James, and of Roseingrave. John Worgan became Organist of St. Andrew's, Undershaft, and St. John's Chapel, Bedford Row. In 1731 he succeeded his brother as Organist at Vauxhall, and in 1753 at St. Botolph's. He proceeded Mus. Doc. in 1775. He died in 1794. He was an excellent Organist, and was coupled by Dr. Wesley with Handel in the following line: " Let Handel or Worgan go thresh at the organ." His compositions include an anthem, two oratorios, songs for Vauxhall, Psalm tunes, glees, and organ and harpsichord music.

1749.

Mus. Doc.—William Boyce. Born in 1710; was educated at St. Paul's School, and was a chorister of St. Paul's, under Charles King. He was afterwards articled to Maurice Greene. In 1734 he became Organist of Oxford Chapel, Vere Street, now St. Peter's. He was at this time a pupil of Dr. Pepusch, and had a wide reputation as a teacher of the harpsichord. In 1736 he succeeded Kelway at St. Michael's, Cornhill, and was in the same year sworn in as composer to the Royal Chapel. In 1737 he was appointed Conductor of the Three Choirs Festival. In 1749 the degree of Mus. Doc. was conferred on him, on the occasion of the installation of the Duke of Newcastle as Chancellor of the University of Cambridge, for which ceremony he composed music to Mason's Ode. On the following day an anthem by him, with orchestral accompaniments, was performed at St. Mary's Church as his exercise. In the same year he became Organist of All Hallows', Thames Street. In 1755 he succeeded Greene as Master of the King's Band, and Conductor of the Festival of the Sons of the Clergy. He suffered all his life from deafness, and this increased so much, that in 1758 he retired to Kensington, where he occupied himself with editing his famous " Cathedral Music," the materials for which had been left him by Greene. The first volume was published in 1760. He died in 1779, and was buried under the dome of St. Paul's. His compositions are very numerous, and take an important place in English music. His masque "Peleus and Thetis" was performed by the Philharmonic Society in 1734, his Oratorio "David's Lamentation over Saul and Jonathan" by the Apollo Society in 1736. His best-known work is a serenata, "Solomon," composed in 1743. Among his other works are twelve Sonatas for two violins and cello, or harpsichord; "Lyra Britannica," a collection of songs and cantatas, in six volumes; several masques and operettas; a large number of Odes for the King's birthday and New-Year's Day are preserved in the Music School at Oxford; anthems and additional accompaniments to Shakespeare's plays. "Hearts of Oak" is one of his songs.

1756.

Mus. Doc.—John Randall, King's Coll. *See* p. 133.

1757.

Mus. Bac.—John Buswell. In the British Museum there is a song, "Where now are all my flattering dreams?" by "Mr. Buswell," to which is appended in MS. the following note: "Of the Chapel Royal, afterwards Mus. Doc." He incorporated at Oxford in 1759.

Mus. Bac.—William Tireman, Organist of Trinity College.

Mus. Doc.—James Nares, non-Coll. Born in 1715, and was a Chorister of the Chapel Royal under Bernard Gates. He also studied under Pepusch. He was Deputy to Piggott at St. George's, Windsor, and in 1734 succeeded Salisbury as Organist of York Minster. In 1756 he succeeded Dr. Greene as Organist and Composer to the Chapel Royal, and succeeded Gates as Master of the Children in 1757. He died in 1783, and was buried at St. Margaret's, Westminster. His compositions are several sets of harpsichord lessons, two treatises on singing, an introduction to playing on the harpsichord and organ, a dramatic ode, the "Royal pastoral," a collection of catches, &c., some organ fugues, anthems, and services.

1758.

Mus. Bac.—Richard Guise.
Mus. Doc.—John Buswell.

1763.

Mus. Doc.—John Stephens. Was a chorister in Gloucester Cathedral, and succeeded Edward Thomson, as Organist of Salisbury, in 1746. He conducted the Gloucester Festival in 1766. He died in 1780. A volume of his Cathedral Music was published in 1805, edited by Highmore Skeats.

1769.

Mus. Doc.—Samuel Howard, of King's College. Born in 1710; was a chorister of the Chapel Royal under Croft, and afterwards a pupil of Pepusch. He was Organist of St. Clement Dane's, Strand, and St. Bride's, Fleet Street. He died in 1782. He composed much operatic and incidental music for theatres, some anthems and hymn tunes, many songs, some of which had an accompaniment for harpsichord and violin. He also assisted Boyce in the compilation of his "Cathedral Music."

1775.

Mus. Doc.—John Worgan. *See* p. 134.

Mus. Doc.—Benjamin Cooke, of Trinity College. Born in 1734; was trained under Dr. Pepusch. At twelve years old he was appointed Deputy to Robinson, Organist of Westminster Abbey. In 1752 he succeeded Pepusch as Conductor of the Academy of Ancient Music, and, in 1762, Robinson as Organist of Westminster Abbey. His degree exercise was an anthem, "Behold now how good and joyful," which had been written for the installation of the Duke of York as a Knight of the Bath. In 1782 he was created Doctor in Music, at Oxford, *honoris causâ*, and in the same year competed successfully with Burney for the post of Organist of St. Martin's-in-the-Fields. He was a member of the "Graduates' Meeting" Club.* He died in 1793, and was buried in the Cloisters of Westminster Abbey. The Library of the Royal College of Music contains MSS. of a large number of his compositions, many of which were written for the Academy of Ancient Music.

---

* App. U.

1775.

Mus. Bac.—Richard Bellamy. Born about 1743. He was appointed a Gentleman of the Chapel Royal in 1771, and Lay Vicar of Westminster Abbey two years later. In 1777 he became a Vicar-Choral of St. Paul's; and, in 1793, Almoner and Master of the children. He was one of the principal bass singers of his day. He published a few sonatas and glees, and a Te Deum with orchestral accompaniment. He died in 1813.

1784.

Mus. Bac.—Robert Hudson, of Trinity College. Born in 1731. Having a tenor voice, he sang in concerts at Ranelagh and Marylebone Gardens. In 1755 he became Assistant-Organist at St. Mildred's, Bread Street, in 1756 Vicar-Choral of St. Paul's, and in 1758 a Gentleman of the Chapel Royal. In 1773 he became Almoner and Master of the children of St. Paul's. He died in 1815, and was buried at St. Paul's. He composed a Cathedral Service, some chants and hymn tunes, and a collection of songs called the "Myrtle" in 1762.

Mus. Doc.—Edmund Ayrton, of Trinity College. One of a family of musicians living at Ripon, where he was born in 1734. He was trained under Dr. Nares at York Minster. He succeeded William Lee as Organist of Southwell Minster in 1754, became a Gentleman of the Chapel Royal in 1764, and afterwards Vicar-Choral of St. Paul's and Lay Vicar of Westminster Abbey. He succeeded Nares as Master of the children of the Chapel Royal in 1780. The exercise for his degree was an anthem, which was performed in Great St. Mary's Church, and afterwards at St. Paul's, in London, at the Peace Thanksgiving of 1784. He is said to have incorporated at Oxford as Doctor of Music in 1788.[*] He died in 1808, and was buried in the Cloisters of Westminster Abbey.

1786.

Mus. Doc.—Edward Miller, of Pembroke Hall. Born in 1731, and was a pupil of Dr. Burney. He was appointed Organist of Doncaster in 1756, on the recommendation of Nares. He

---

[*] See Foster's "Alumni Oxonienses."

died in 1807. His compositions include elegies, songs, music for the harpsichord and flute, Psalm tunes, &c., "The Elements of Thorough Bass and Composition," and he also wrote a History of Doncaster.

1794.

Mus. Bac.—Charles Hague, of Trinity Hall. Born in Yorkshire in 1769; he studied the violin at Cambridge under Manini, and composition under Hellendaal the elder. Manini died in 1785, and Hague went to London and studied under Salomon and Dr. Cooke. After returning to Cambridge, Crotch became one of his pupils. He succeeded Dr Randall in 1799 as Professor of Music, and in 1801 proceeded Doctor of Music. He died in 1821. The exercise for his Bachelor's degree was an anthem, "By the Waters of Babylon." Other compositions were glees, and an Ode for the installation of the Duke of Gloucester as Chancellor. He also arranged some symphonies of Haydn, and, in conjunction with Plumptre, Fellow of Clare, a collection of songs.

1799.

Mus. Doc.—Clarke-Whitfeld. *See* p. 95.

1801.

Mus. Doc.—Charles Hague.

Mus. Doc.—Thomas Busby, of Magd., also LL.D. Born in 1755; studied singing under Champness, and the harpsichord under Knyvett and Battishill. He was, however, more successful with literature than with music, and was connected with the *London Courant, Morning Post*, and several other papers. About 1780 he was appointed Organist of St. Mary Newington, and was employed as a teacher of Latin, French, and music. In 1786 he and Arnold brought out a musical dictionary. Busby afterwards issued "The Divine Harmonist," containing selections from musical works by himself and others. In 1798 he was appointed Organist of St. Mary, Woolnoth. In 1799 his Oratorio "The Prophecy" was produced by Cramer. In 1801 his secular Oratorio "Brittania" was performed at Covent Garden, Mara singing the principal soprano part. About 1800 be brought out a

"New and Complete Musical Dictionary," and started the "Monthly Musical Journal," the first English musical periodical. His degree exercise was a "Thanksgiving Ode on the Naval Victories." His translation of Lucretius into English verse was published in 1813. In the latter part of his life he brought out a grammar of music, a dictionary of musical terms, and in 1819 his "History of Music," a compilation from Burney and Hawkins. He died in 1838. "He was not an original genius, but a clever, hard-working man of letters."—*Dict. Nat. Biog.*

1805.

Mus. Bac.—William Carnaby, Trinity Hall. Born in 1772, was a Chorister of the Chapel Royal under Nares and Ayrton, and afterwards Organist of Eye and Huntingdon. He proceeded Doctor of Music in 1808. In 1823 he became Organist of Hanover Chapel, Regent Street, which post he occupied until his death in 1839. His compositions "are respectable and meritorious, if not remarkably original."—*Dict. Nat. Biog.*

1808.

Mus. Bac.—Joseph Kemp, of Sidney Sussex Coll. Born in 1778, a theorist and composer, was educated under W. Jackson, Organist of Exeter. He proceeded Mus. Doc. in 1809. He wrote a number of songs, anthems, chants, &c. His degree exercises were: a War anthem, "A sound of battle is in the land," for the Bachelor, and an anthem, "The Crucifixion," for the Doctor. He was Organist of Bristol Cathedral from 1802 to 1809. He died in 1824.

Mus. Doc.—William Carnaby, Trinity Hall.

1809.

Mus. Doc.—Joseph Kemp, Sidney.

1811.

Mus. Bac.—George Augustus Polgreen Bridgetower, a Mulatto, of Trinity Hall. A violinist, who is perhaps best known as having been the first to perform Beethoven's "Kreutzer" Sonata, and to whom it is said to have been originally dedicated. He was born in Poland in 1779, and made his first appearance in London, at Drury Lane Theatre, on February 19, 1790. In 1791 he and Hummel, dressed in scarlet coats, pulled the stops for Joah Bates, while playing the organ at the Handel commemoration in Westminster Abbey. In 1802 he went to Dresden, where he gave very successful concerts. The next year he became acquainted with Beethoven, who wrote the "Kreutzer" Sonata for him and played it with him.* The last we hear of him is that he took the degree of Bachelor in Music in 1811, his exercise consisting of an anthem, with words by F. A. Rawdon, which was performed, with full orchestra and chorus, at Great St. Mary's, on June 30. He is believed to have died in 1850.

Mus. Doc.—John George Henry Jay, of Trinity Hall. Was born in 1770, and studied the violin and composition abroad. He matriculated at Magdalen Hall, Oxford, in 1809, but did not take a degree at that University. He settled in London till his death in 1849. His published compositions are music for the piano, piano and flute, a song, and a Hungarian duet.

1812.

Mus. Bac.—John Camidge, St. Catherine's. Born in 1790; was a pupil and assistant of his father, Mathew, and grandson of John the elder, both of whom were Organists of York Minster. He was an excellent organist, and succeeded his father at York Minster in 1842. He proceeded Doctor of Music in 1819. He published a volume of Cathedral music, and adapted much classical music to the English service. After the fire of 1829 he superintended the building of the new organ, which was considered one of the finest in the world. He died in 1859, after having been paralysed for eleven years.

1812.

Mus. Doc.—George William Chard, St. Catherine's. Born about 1765, was appointed Assistant-Organist and Lay Clerk at Winchester Cathedral in 1787, and Organist in 1802. He became Organist of Winchester College in 1832. He died in 1849. His compositions are unimportant.

---

* At the Augarten-Halle, Vienna, in May, 1803.

1819.

Mus. Doc.—John Camidge, St. Cath. *See* p. 140.

1825.

Mus. Doc.—Edward Hodges, Sidney Sussex. Born in 1796. Was Organist of Clifton Church, and afterwards of St. James and St. Nicholas at Bristol. In 1838 he was appointed Organist of St. John's Church, New York, and in 1846 of Trinity. In 1863 he returned to Clifton, where he died in 1867. He published a service, two anthems, some hymn tunes, and some writings on church music.

1828.

Mus. Bac.—Samuel Mathews, Trinity College.*

1833.

Mus. Bac.—Thomas Attwood Walmisley, Jesus Coll. B.A., 1838; M.A., 1841; Mus. Doc., 1848. Born in 1814; was a godson and pupil of Attwood. He early developed technical facility, and in after-life became an able exponent of Bach's Fugues and Beethoven's Sonatas. In 1830 he was appointed Organist of Croydon Church, and in 1833 Organist of Trinity and St. John's Colleges, Cambridge. His Bachelor's exercise was "Let God arise," an anthem with full orchestra. He entered at Corpus, but migrated to Jesus. At this time he was playing the organ twice every Sunday at each of the following places: King's, the University Church, Trinity, and St. John's, making eight services altogether. He succeeded Clarke-Whitfeld as Professor of Music in 1836, while he was still in residence for his B.A. degree. He twice composed Odes for the installation of Chancellors, one being for that of the Prince Consort. He proceeded Doctor of Music in 1848, and continued his work at Cambridge till his death in 1856. He was one of the chief English organists of his day, and his compositions for the Church are excellent. In knowledge of musical history and general cultivation he was in advance of most English musicians. He was one of the first to inaugurate musical lectures with practical examples. He was

---

* This is the first Degree in Music entered in the University Calendar.

on intimate terms with Mendelssohn, and did his best at Cambridge to inculcate the teaching of the latter with regard to Bach's music. His published works are his two odes, anthems, services, and songs, and in MS. there are some duets for pianoforte and oboe.

1836.

Mus. Bac.—Edward Dearle, of Queen's College. Mus. Doc., 1842.

1842.

Mus. Bac.—John Larkin Hopkins, of St. John's College. Born in 1819; was a Chorister in Westminster Abbey under Turle. In 1841 he succeeded R. Banks as Organist of Rochester Cathedral; in 1856 he became Organist of Trinity College, Cambridge. He proceeded Doctor of Music in 1857. He died at Ventnor in 1873. He composed glees and madrigals, services, anthems, and carols.

Mus. Doc.—Edward Dearle, Queen's Coll.

1848.

Mus. Doc.—Thomas Attwood Walmisley, Trinity Coll. *See* p. 141.

1849.

Mus. Doc.—William Richard Bexfield, Trinity College. Mus. Bac., Oxon., 1846. *See* p. 104.

1851.

Mus. Bac. and Mus. Doc.—Henry Wylde, of Trinity College. Born in 1822; studied under Moscheles and Cipriani Potter, and was afterwards a Professor at the Royal Academy of Music. In 1863 he was elected Gresham Professor, in succession to Edward Taylor. He was one of the founders, and afterwards conductor, of the New Philharmonic Society in 1852. He founded the London Academy of Music, and built St. George's Hall in 1867 for this purpose. His compositions include a setting of Milton's " Paradise Lost," a cantata, piano works, and works on musical theory. He died in 1890.

Mus. Bac. and Mus. Doc.—Charles Steggall.

1856.

Mus. Doc.—William Sterndale Bennett, of St. John's College. Born in 1816; son of Robert Bennett, Organist of the Parish Church of Sheffield. In 1824 he became a Chorister at King's College, Cambridge, and studied under his grandfather, who was Lay Clerk of King's, St. John's, and Trinity. In 1826 he entered the Royal Academy of Music as a violin student, and afterwards studied the piano under W. H. Holmes, Cipriani Potter, and Crotch. He also occasionally sang in St. Paul's Cathedral, until his voice broke. His genius for composition developed rapidly, and in 1832 his first and second symphonies, his first concerto, and the overture to the "Tempest" were completed. The performance of his first concerto brought him under the notice of Mendelssohn, with whom he contracted a firm friendship, and whose influence on his music has led to the belief that Bennett became his pupil, which, however, was never the case. In 1834 Bennett became Organist of Wandsworth Church, a post he soon discarded. In 1836 he went to the Lower Rhine Festival at Düsseldorf, where Mendelssohn renewed acquaintance with him; and from there he went, at Mendelssohn's invitation, to Leipsic, where he met Schumann. One result of his visit to the Rhine was the composition of his "Naiads" Overture. On January 19, 1837, he played one of his concertos at the Gewandhaus, and on February 13 his "Naiads" was produced there. After his return to England he became one of the Professors of the Royal Academy of Music, and in 1866 its Principal. He frequently revisited Germany, and in 1842 made the acquaintance, at Cassel, of Spohr and Hauptmann. In 1854 he conducted the first performance in England of Bach's "St. Matthew Passion," at Hanover Square Rooms, under the auspices of the Bach Society, which had been founded in 1849. In 1856 he succeeded Walmisley as Professor of Music at Cambridge, and was created Mus. Doc. in the same year and M.A. in 1867. Up to this time the regulations for admission to degrees in music had been very lax: Bennett, therefore, instituted an examination, and took other measures for the cultivation of music in the University. Composition was not neglected during these years, and some of the chief works produced were the "May Queen" (at Leeds, in 1858), the "Exhibition Ode," "Ode on the Installation of the Duke of Devonshire" as Chancellor of the University of Cambridge, and the Overture to "Paradise and the Peri" in 1862. In 1864 the Symphony in G minor was produced by the Philharmonic Society, and in 1865 was performed at the Gewandhaus. The "Woman of Samaria" was produced at Birmingham in 1867, and in 1872 he composed music to the "Ajax," his last important work. In addition to the Cambridge degrees, Bennett received the degree of D.C.L. at Oxford, *honoris causâ*, in 1870.* He was knighted at Windsor in 1871. He died on January 24, 1875, aged 59, and was buried at Westminster Abbey. For an excellent notice of his life and works, see "Dict. Nat. Biog.," from which the above sketch is taken.

1857.

Mus. Bac.—Edward Bunnett, Corpus Christi College. Mus. Doc., 1869.

Mus. Bac.— George Mursell Garrett, St. John's College. Mus. Doc., 1867; M.A. by grace of the Senate, 1878, being the first musician upon whom this degree has been conferred without residence, with the exception of the Professors of Music.

1859.

Mus. Bac.—Edmund Thomas Chipp, of St. John's College. Born in 1823; son of the famous drummer, T. P. Chipp. He was educated as a chorister of the Chapel Royal, under W. Hawes. He also studied the violin, and was a member of the Queen's private band, and the orchestras of the Italian Opera and Philharmonic Society. After holding successively a number of appointments as organist in London, he went to Belfast in 1862, where he also held several appointments as organist. He proceeded Mus. Doc. in 1861. In 1866 he went to Scotland, and became successively organist at Dundee and Edinburgh. At the end of 1866 he was appointed Organist of Ely Cathedral, where he remained

---

* Degrees in Music were not granted at Oxford *honoris causâ* until 1879.

till his death, which took place at Nice in 1886. He composed two short oratorios, "Naomi" and "Job," and some songs, organ and pianoforte music, and services.

1861.
Mus. Doc.—Edmund Thomas Chipp, of St. John's Coll. *See* p. 144.

1863.
Mus. Bac.—Alfred Robert Gaul, St. John's Coll.

1864.
Mus. Bac.—Langdon Colborne, Trin. Coll. Born in 1837. Was elected Organist of St. Michael's College, Tenbury, in 1860. In 1874 he became Organist of Beverley Minster, and in 1877 of Hereford Cathedral. He graduated Mus. Doc., Lambeth, in 1883. His compositions consist of church music, part-songs, and songs. Died 1889.

1865.
Mus. Bac.—Thomas Anderton, St. John's Coll.
Mus. Bac.—Richard William Crowe. Mus. Doc., 1872.
Mus. Bac.—John Bradbury Turner, St. John's Coll.
Mus. Bac.—Carl Oscar Waldemar Malmène, St. John's Coll.

1867.
Mus. Bac.—Frederick Cook Atkinson, St. John's Coll.
Mus. Bac.—Robert Lindley Nunn, St. John's Coll.
Mus. Doc.—George Mursell Garrett, St. John's Coll. *See* p. 144.
Mus. Doc.—John Larkin Hopkins, St. John's Coll. *See* p. 142.

1869.
Mus. Bac.—Horace Hill, St. John's Coll. Mus. Doc., 1878.
Mus. Doc.—Edward Bunnett, of Trinity Coll., previously of Corpus.

1871.
Mus. Bac.—Charles Swinnerton Heap, St. John's Coll. Mus. Doc., 1872.
Mus. Bac.—Charles John Blood Meacham, St. John's Coll.
Mus. Bac.—Joseph Parry, St. John's Coll. Mus. Doc., 1878.
Mus. Bac.—Herbert Warren, Trinity Coll.
Mus. Doc., *Honoris causâ.*—Sir Herbert Oakeley. *See* p. 114.

1872.

Mus. Bac.—Edwin John Crow, St. John's Coll. Mus. Doc., 1882.
Mus. Doc.—Richard William Crowe, St. John's Coll.
Mus. Doc.—Charles Swinnerton Heap, St. John's Coll.

1873.

Mus. Bac.—Arthur Carnall, St. John's Coll.
Mus. Bac.—Samuel Corbett, St. John's Coll. Mus. Doc., 1879.
Mus. Bac.—Samuel Weekes, St. John's Coll.

1875.

Mus. Bac. and Mus. Doc.—George Alexander Macfarren, Trinity Coll., created Doctor in Music on his appointment of Professor, in succession to Sir W. Sterndale Bennett. He was born in 1813, and was a student at the Royal Academy of Music, of which he became a Professor in 1834, and Principal in 1875. His first important work was a Symphony in C, produced at the Royal Academy in 1830. After this he produced Symphonies in D minor, 1831; in F minor, 1834; Overture in D, 1831; music to the "Maid of Switzerland," 1832; his Overture "Chevy Chase," 1836 (produced by Mendelssohn at the Gewandhaus in 1843); "Devil's Opera" in 1838, at the Lyceum; and many other works, besides editing several of the works of Handel and Purcell. In later life he became blind, but still continued his activity, producing the oratorios "St. John the Baptist," at Bristol, in 1873; "The Resurrection," at Birmingham, in 1876; "Joseph," at Leeds, 1877; music to "Ajax," 1882; "King David," at Leeds, 1883; besides smaller works. He also published several important and well-known works on the theory of music, and among his pupils are many of our most eminent musicians. He graduated M.A. in 1878, and was knighted in 1883. The degree of Mus. Doc., *honoris causâ*, was conferred on him at Oxford in 1876, and at Dublin in 1887. His last published composition was an Andante and Rondo for violin and organ, contained in the *Organist's Quarterly Journal* for October, 1887. He died on October 31, 1887.

1876.

Mus. Bac.—Henry Fisher, St. John's Coll. Mus. Doc., 1878.
Mus. Bac.—Henry Cotter Nixon, Trinity Coll.
Mus. Bac.—Francis Edward Gladstone, St. John's Coll. Mus. Doc., 1879.
Mus. Bac.—John Shepherd Liddle, St. John's Coll.
Mus. Bac.—George Marsden, St. John's Coll. Mus. Doc., 1882.
Mus. Bac.—William Joseph Westbrook, Queen's Coll. Mus. Doc., 1878.
Mus. Doc., *Honoris causâ.*—Arthur Seymour Sullivan, Trin. Coll. Created Mus. Doc., Oxon., *honoris causâ*, in 1879. Knighted in 1883.
Mus. Doc., *Honoris causâ.*—Sir John Goss, Trinity College. Born in 1800, was a pupil of Attwood, whom, in 1838, he succeeded as Organist of St. Paul's. In 1856 Goss succeeded Knyvett as one of the Composers to the Chapel Royal. He was knighted in 1872. His anthems, services, and other works for the Church are well known, and he was also the composer of songs, glees, and orchestral pieces. His book on "Harmony and Thorough-bass," published in 1847, had, in 1879, reached its thirteenth edition. He died in 1880.

1877.

Mus. Bac.—John Morgan Bentley, Downing Coll. Mus. Doc., 1879.
Mus. Bac.—Charles Joseph Frost, Sidney Sussex Coll. Mus. Doc., 1882.
Mus. Bac.—Walter Edward Lawson, Queen's Coll.
Mus. Bac.—George Oakey, St. John's Coll.
Mus. Bac.—Edwin Charles Such, Trinity Coll.
Mus. Bac.—Horton Claridge Allison, St. John's Coll. Proceeded Mus. Doc. at Dublin in 1877.
Mus. Doc., *Honoris causâ.*—Joseph Joachim, of Trinity College.

1878.

Mus. Bac.—John Asquith, St. John's Coll.
Mus. Bac.—George Benson, St. John's Coll. Died 1884.
Mus. Bac.—Alfred James Caldicott, Trinity Coll.
Mus. Bac.—James Dawber, St. John's Coll.
Mus. Bac.—David Jenkins, St. John's Coll.

Mus. Bac.—Walter Henry Nichols, Queen's Coll.
Mus. Bac.—Walter Stokes, St. John's Coll. Mus. Doc., 1882.
Mus. Doc.—Henry Fisher, St. John's Coll.
Mus. Doc.—Horace Hill, St. John's Coll.
Mus. Doc.—Joseph Parry, St. John's Coll.
Mus. Doc.—William Joseph Westbrook, Queen's Coll.

1879.

Mus. Bac.—James Pattinson.
Mus. Doc.—John Morgan Bentley, Downing Coll.
Mus. Doc.—Samuel Corbett, St. John's Coll.
Mus. Doc.—Francis Edward Gladstone, St. John's Coll.

1880.

Mus. Bac.—Nicholas Kilburn.
Mus. Bac.—George Shinn.
Mus. Bac.—John Taylor, St. John's Coll.
Mus. Bac.—James Turpin.
Mus. Bac.—Charles Chambers. Mus. Doc., 1887.
Mus. Bac.—William Skinner Vinning, Trinity Coll.

1881.

Mus. Bac.—Charles William Pearce. Mus. Doc., 1884.

1882.

Mus. Bac.—Ralph Dunstan. Mus. Doc., 1892.
Mus. Bac.—Thomas Hirst Fall.
Mus. Bac.—Richard Stokoe, Emmanuel.
Mus. Bac.—William Henry Tutt.
Mus. Bac.—Herbert Walter Wareing. Mus. Doc., 1886.
Mus. Bac.—Henry Watson, St. John's Coll. Mus. Doc., 1887.
Mus. Bac.—Morton Latham, Trinity Coll. B.A., 1865 ; M.A., 1882.
Mus. Bac.—Arthur Edmonds Crook.
Mus. Bac.—Henry Halton.
Mus. Bac.—Henry Stevens, St. John's Coll.
Mus. Bac.—Charles Hage Briggs. Mus. Doc., 1885.
Mus. Bac.—John Henry Roberts.
Mus. Doc.—Edwin John Crow, St. John's Coll.
Mus. Doc.—Charles Joseph Frost, Sidney Sussex Coll.
Mus. Doc.—Walter Stokes, St. John's Coll.

1883.

Mus. Bac.—Arthur Francis Smith, Queen's Coll.
Mus. Doc., *Honoris causâ.*—Charles Hubert Hastings Parry, Trinity Coll. *See* p. 109.

1884.

Mus. Bac.—Joshua Ives, Queen's Coll.
Mus. Bac.—William John Leaver, St. John's Coll.
Mus. Bac.—Edward Hulton Middleton, St. John's Coll. Mus. Doc., 1887.
Mus. Bac.—John Robertson, St. John's Coll.
Mus. Doc.—Charles William Pearce.

1885.

Mus. Bac.—William Clark Ainley.
Mus. Bac.—Arthur James Greenish. Mus. Doc., 1892.
Mus. Bac.—Frederick James Karn.
Mus. Bac.—Thomas Lee.
Mus. Bac.—Felix Wilson Morley, Pembroke Coll. B.A., 1878; M.A., 1883.
Mus. Bac.—James Sneddon, St. John's Coll.
Mus. Bac.—Frederick James.
Mus. Bac.—George Herbert Robinson, Trinity Coll.
Mus. Bac.—Frank Osmond Carr, Trinity Coll. B.A., 1883; M.A., 1886; Mus. Bac., Oxon., 1884; Mus. Doc., Oxon., 1891.
Mus. Doc.—Charles Hage Briggs.

1886.

Mus. Bac.—Charles Wilson Fisher, St. John's Coll.
Mus Bac.—Alan Gray, Trinity Coll. LL.B., 1877; LL.M., 1883; Mus. Doc., 1889.
Mus. Bac.—Frederick Dewberry, Gonville and Caius Coll.
Mus. Bac.—James Alcock.
Mus. Bac.—William Henry Barrow.
Mus. Bac.—William Darby.
Mus. Bac.—Thomas Isaac Watts, Queen's Coll. B.A., 1887; M.A., 1891.
Mus. Bac.—Isaiah Roper, King's Coll.
Mus. Doc.—Herbert Walter Wareing, King's Coll.

1887.

Mus. Bac.—William Charles Dewberry, Christ's.
Mus. Bac.—William Henry Hannaford.
Mus. Bac.—Alfred Mayo.
Mus. Bac.—Henry Piggott.
Mus. Bac.—Richard James Everett Hopper.
Mus. Bac.—Hugh Blair, Christ's Coll. B.A., 1886.
Mus. Bac.—Frederick Robert Frye.
Mus. Bac.—Frederick Kilvington Hattersley.
Mus. Bac.—George Frederic Huntley, Trinity Coll.
Mus. Bac.—Thomas Johnson, St. John's Coll.
Mus. Bac.—Henry Newboult.
Mus. Bac.—Arthur William Wiseman, Gonville and Caius Coll. B.A., 1884; M.A., 1887.
Mus. Doc.—Edward Hulton Middleton, St. John's Coll.
Mus. Doc.—Henry Watson, St. John's Coll.
Mus. Doc.—Charles Chambers.

1888.

Mus. Bac.—Frederic Leeds.
Mus. Bac.—Walter Thomas Southward, St. Catharine's Coll. B.A., 1875; M.A., 1878.
Mus. Bac.—George John Bennett, Trinity Coll. Mus. Doc., 1893.
Mus. Doc., by Grace of the Senate.—Charles Villiers Stanford, Trinity Coll. B.A., 1874; M.A., 1877; Mus. Doc., Oxon., 1883; Professor of Music, 1887.
Mus. Doc., *Honoris causâ.*—Alexander Campbell Mackenzie.

1889.

Mus. Doc.—Alan Gray, Trinity Coll.

1890.

Mus. Bac.—Charles Wood, Gonville and Caius Coll. B.A., 1890.
Mus. Bac.—William Henry Speer, Trinity Coll. B.A., 1886; M.A., 1890.
Mus. Bac.—Richard John Farrell, Downing Coll.
Mus. Bac.—Herbert Arthur Wheeldon.
Mus. Bac.—Charles Stanley Wise.

1891.

Mus. Bac.—Charles Thomas Corke, Trinity Coll.
Mus. Bac.—Edward Woodall Naylor, Emmanuel Coll. B.A., 1887; M.A., 1891.
Mus. Bac.—Robert Henry Turner, Corpus Christi Coll. B.A., 1883; M.A., 1886.
Mus. Bac.—Lawrence Walker.
Mus. Bac.—Arthur Murray Goodhart, King's Coll. B.A., 1888.
Mus. Bac.—Charles Francis Abdy Williams, Trinity Hall. B.A., 1879; M.A., 1882; Mus. B., Oxon., 1889.
Mus. Doc. *Honoris causâ.*—Anton Dvorák.

1892.

Mus. Bac.—George John Miller.
Mus. Bac.—Henry Walford Davies.
Mus. Bac.—Freeman Whatmoor.
Mus. Bac.—Charles Legh Naylor, Emmanuel Coll.
Mus. Bac.—Herbert Compigné Andrews, St. John's Coll.
Mus. Bac.—Henry Taylor.
Mus. Doc.—Ralph Dunstan.
Mus. Doc.—Arthur James Greenish.

1893.

Mus. Bac.—Thomas Berry.
Mus. Bac.—William Haydn Cox.
Mus. Bac.—James Richard Washington.
Mus. Doc.—George John Bennett, Trinity Coll.

HONORARY DEGREES.

Mus. Doc.—Charles Camille Saint-Saëns.
Mus. Doc.—Max Christian Friedrich Bruch.
Mus. Doc.—Pierre Ilitsch Tschaikowsky. Died Nov. 6, 1893.
Mus. Doc.—Antonio Arrigo Boito.
Edvard Grieg was prevented by illness from presenting himself for this degree.

APPENDIX.

A.

The following persons are mentioned in history as graduates in music, but no record of their degrees has been found in the University registers:—

Mus. Doc.—John Hamboys. Flourished 1470. See p. 15.

Mus. Bac.—John Floyd, a Gentleman of the Chapel of Henry VIII., who made a pilgrimage to Jerusalem. After his return, he died in the King's Chapel, and was buried in the Savoy Church; and the following inscription was placed on his tomb: "Johannes Floyd, virtutis et religionis cultor. Obiit 3 Ap. 1523."* There is a composition by him in the British Museum. Add. MSS. 31,922.

Mus. Bac.—Ambrose Payne. "Of your charity pray for the soul of Sir Ambrose Payne, Parson of Lambeth and Bachelor of Music, and Chapleyn to the lords Cardinals Bonsar and Morton, who departed May the XXVIII., A.D. 1528." This inscription was found on a tombstone in Lambeth Parish Church.†

Mus. Doc.—Musgrave Heighington. Born in 1680; was organist of Yarmouth, and afterwards of Leicester. He apparently practised the profession of music at Dublin for some time. His compositions are six select odes and music to "The Enchanter, or Harlequin Merlin," a pantomime published at Dublin. It is not known at which University he graduated.

Mus. Bac.—George Marson, one of the contributors to "The Triumphs of Oriana," in 1601. Some of his services and anthems are extant in MS.

---

* Hawkins, p. 522. † Hawkins, p. 291.

Mus. Bac.—Thomas Hunt; contributed to "The Triumphs of Oriana." The Barnard MS. Collection contains an anthem by him.

B.

1463. Item, admissus fuit Henricus Abyngton in musica bachalaureus, 22 die Febr. cuius communa 20d.—Cambridge Grace Book, A., p. 28a.

C.

1463. Concessa est gracia Henrico Habyngton quod post admissionem ad gradum bachalarii (sic) in Musica, possit admitti ad incipiendum in eadem sic quod continuet hic ante admissionem per annum.—Cambridge Grace Book, A., p. 30b.

D.

A.D. 1463. Ann. 3 Ed. IV. Pro Doctore Musicæ. Rex omnibus ad quos, &c., salutem. Sciatis quod de gratia nostra speciali concessimus dilecto et fideli capellano nostro magistro Thome Saintviste Doctori Musicæ quod ipse sit magister Collegii nostri in Cantabrigia, the Kynges Hall vulgariter nuncupati, habendum occupandum et gaudendum per se vel deputatum suum sufficientem pro termino vitiæ ipsius Thome cum omnibus proficuis commoditatibus et emolumentis ad idem spectantibus sive aliquo modo pertinentibus. In cujus, &c. Teste rege apud Pountfret duodecimo die decembris. Per ipsum regem et de data prædicta, &c. (Rymer, Fœdera, Ed. 1710, ann. 1463. Vol. XI., p. 510).

E.

1470. Concessa est gratia Lessy de capella Ducisse Ebor, vt cum studio et speculacione in musica et cum practica eiusdem possit intrare in musica.—Cambridge Grace Book, A., p. 65b.

F.

Conceditur Humfrido Fryvell vt studium 2 annorum in musica in ista vniuersitate cum practica quinque annorum in eadem in patria sufficiat sibi ad intrandum in eadem. From Registrum Magistrorum Jacobi Denton et Th. Gogney, 1495-96.—Cambridge Grace Book, B., p. 99.

1505. Item, conceditur magistro Humfrido Frevill bacallario in musica vt studium trium annorum in hac vniuersitate et in patria sibi stent pro completa forma ad incipiendum in musica. —Cambridge Grace Book, Γ, p. 22*a*.

G.

1501-2. Item, conceditur magistro Fayerfax erudito in musica quod post gradum bacallariatus sua erudicione possit stare pro forma ad incipiendum in musica. — Cambridge Grace Book, Γ, p. 2*b*.

1502. Item, conceditur magistro Wydow Bacallario in musica Oxonie, quod possit stare eodum et incorporari hic et vti habitu suo gradui competenti cuiuscunque coloris velit.—Cambridge Grace Book, Γ, p. 5*a*.

H.

1502. Item, conceditur magistro Roberto Cowper vt studium quinque annorum cum practica totidem annorum citra introitum suum in eadem sufficiat sibi ad incipiendum in musica. — *Ibid.*, p. 3*a*.

1503. Item, conceditur Johanni Parker vt studium trium annorum et dimidium in hac vniuersitate in arte musica sufficiat sibi pro completa forma ad intrandum in eadem arte.—*Ibid.*, p. 8*b*.

21 Ap. 1516. Mgr. Robertus Coper Musices Doctor ad ecclesiam de Est Aersley in Decm. de Croydon, *ex Coll. Archiep.*

23 Maii, 1516. Mag. Robtus Cooper, in Musiciis Doctor ad eccl. de Lachyndon cum capella annexa in Decm. Bucking., *ex. Coll. Archiep.*—Baker XLI., 219.

I.

1516. Item, conceditur Johanni Watkyns vt studium septem annorum in musica hic et alibi sufficiant sibi ad intrandum in sciencia musicali sic quod missam et antiphonam pro forma componat.—Cambridge Grace Book, Γ, p. 70*b*.

J.

1516. Item, conceditur domino Johanni Firtun sacerdoti vno vicariorum de collegio regali sancti Stephani Westmonastorii vt studium octo annorum in eodem collegio et totidem in capella ducis Norfolk sit sibi sufficiens ad intrandum in sciencia musicali sic quod faciat missam et antiphonam de sancta maria.—Cambridge Grace Book, Γ, p. 70b.

K.

1519. Item, conceditur domino Beniamino Beryderyke vt studium vnius anni in speculacione musice hic in academia et quinque in quibus practicauit et docuit in patria sufficiant sibi ad intrandum in eadem facultate sic quod componat missam beate marie.—*Ibid.*, p. 94b.

L.

1536. In primis conceditur Cristofero Tye vt studium decem annorum in arte musica cum practica multa in eadem, tum componendo, tum pueros erudiendo, sufficiat ei ad intrandum in eadem, sic vt componat vnam missam vel paulo post comitia canendam, vel eo ipso die quo serenissimi principis obseruabitur aduentus, saltem vt manifestum ac euidens aliquod specimen eius eruditionis sic ostendat in comitiis.— Cambridge Grace Book, Γ, p. 156b.

M.

1544-5. Item, conceditur Cristofero Tye hic apud vos in musica bacchalaureus (*sic*) vt studium et practica decem annorum post gradum bacchalaureatus susceptum, sufficiat ei pro completo gradu doctoratus in eadem facultate. Ita tamen vt componat missam in die comitiorum canendam coram vobis, conviuet, et satisfaciat officiaris. Et quoniam non reperitur doctor in eadem facultate, presentetur in habitu non regentis per vnum procuratorum.

Item, conceditur eidem nuper admisso ad incipiendum in musica vt possit vti comitiorum tempore habitu doctoris in medicina.—Cambridge Grace Book, Δ, p. 12b.

N.

1560. Conceditur 13 decembris Robto. Wight, vt studium 10 annorum in musica sufficiat ei ad intrandum in eadem, sic tamen vt componat communionem cantandam in ecclesia beate marie coram vniuersitate in die comitiorum sub pena quadraginta solidorum (omnia peregit).—*Ibid.*, p. 60b.

O.

1606. Conceditur Orlando Gibbins regius organista (*sic*) vt studium septem annorum in musica sufficiat ei ad intrandum in eadem, sic tamen vt canticum componat cantandum, hora et loco per vicecancellarium designandis coram vniuersitate in die comitiorum et vt presentetur per magistrum regentem in habitu bacchalaurei in artibus.—Cambridge Grace Book, E., p. 73.

P.

The following inscription to John Tomkins stood in the old Cathedral of St. Paul :*—"Johannes Tomkins, Musicæ Baccalaureus, organista sui temporis celeberrimus, post-quam capellæ regali per annos duodecim, huic autem ecclesiæ per novem decem sedulo inserviisset, ad cœlestem chorum migravit Septembris 27, anno Domini 1638. Ætatis suæ 52. Cujus desiderium mœrens uxor hoc testatur marmore."

Q.

Practicantes in Musica. Conceditur 10 Junij 1616. Supplicat reverentijs vestris Robertus Ramsey vt studium septem annorum in musica sufficiat ei ad intrandum in eadem, sic tamen vt canticum componat cantandum in Ecclesia Beate Marie coram Uniuersitate in die commitiorum, et vt presentetur per magistrum in habitu bacchalaurei in Artibus.—Cambridge Grace Book, E., p. 243.

R.

The Grace creating the Professorship of Music at Cambridge runs as follows : "July 2, 1684. Cum par sit et æquum atque etiam e dignitate Academiæ, ut elegantissima facultas musicæ suum quoque haud secus ac ceteræ professorem habeat :

" Placeat vobis ut senatus auctoritate constituatur musices Professor atque ut ornatissimus vir Dr. Stagins hac vestra gratia in illud munus rite electus nomine et titulo publici vestri in Musica Professoris insigniatur."—Stat. Acad. Cant., 1785, p. 404.

---

* Hawkins, p. 507.

S.

Feb. 10, 1579-80. Supplicat Johannes Lant, publicus musicæ prælector, ut a munere legendi liberetur, et scholares illi qui teneantur interesse musicæ lectioni ad arithmeticam transferrantur. Causa est quod illius lectionis utilitas modica sit auditoribus, et ideo ex more hæc dispensatio concedi solet. A. Clark, "Register Univ. Ox.," Vol. II., p. 100.

T.

Of the Library of Duke Humfrey, 1439. Item, statutum et ordinatum est per eandem Universitatem, quod omnes et singuli libri alias per eundem serenissimum principem pro lectura septem artium liberalium et trium philosophiarum, nec non et per alios ad eundem usum collati seu in futurum conferendi, in quadam cista per vniversitatem ad hoc ordinanda, in communi libraria vniversitatis, sub custodia custodis ejusdem, per indenturas inter dictam vniversitatem et dictum pro tempore custodis exeuntem confectas, reponantur, quæ quidem cista in futuris vocabitur "Cista trium philosophiarum et septem scientiarum liberalium"; ad effectum quod magistris dictas scientias actualiter et publice in scholis artium legentibus seu legere volentibus per indenturas inter dictum custodem et dictos magistros conficiendas, deliberentur, &c. Anstey's "Munimenta Academica," Vol. I., p. 327. There is nothing here to show that Duke Humfrey founded lectureships, or did anything more than supply books for the use of the masters in arts, in order that they should properly perform their statutory duties of reading the "seven liberal sciences" in the schools.

Of the books given by Duke Humfrey, only three remain in the Bodleian Library, the rest having been dispersed or destroyed.

U.

The Graduates' Meeting was a Society of Musical Professors resident in London, which was established on November 24, 1790, at Dr. Arnold's house, 480, Strand, opposite Craven Street. An account of it exists in the British Museum, in the handwriting of Dr. Callcott. Dupuis was the initiator, and among the members were Arnold, Burney, Dupuis, Cooke, Parsons, and Callcott. Meetings were held at intervals at the houses of the members, and it is recorded that "Dr. Haydn," who joined the Society in 1791, gave his dinner at Parsloe's, a Coffee House in St. James Street, on June 20, 1792, and that Salomon was invited to act as interpreter for Haydn. Discords occasionally arose, as, for instance, when a member proposed that no one should be elected to any Cathedral appointment without a testimonial from this Society, which met with so much disapprobation that the proposer retired from the Society; but, on the whole, the objects of friendship and conviviality seem to have been fairly well carried out.

The largest number reached by the members seems to have been fourteen, that being the number of graduates in London soon after its foundation. The Society seems to have died a natural death about the beginning of the present century.—From the *Musical Times*, December, 1892.

INDEX.

Figures in italics refer to the principal notice given concerning the Graduate named.

Abdy, 12.
Abell, 130.
Abernethy, 117.
Abram, *110*, 112.
Abyngton, 15, 17, *119*, 153.
Acoustics, 21, 39.
Act, 9, 21, 27, 28, 30.
Agate, 117.
Agutter, 110.
Ainley, 149.
Alcock, James, 149.
Alcock, John, the elder, *87*, 89.
Alcock, John, the younger, 90.
Alcock, W. B., 114.
Alcuin, 11.
Alderson, M. F , 118.
Aldrich, 49, *note*.
Allchin, 52, *110*.
Allen, G. B., 105.
Allen, J., 77.
Allibond, 4, 35.
Allison, 147.
Amner, *78*, 128.
Amps, 56.
Anderson, 113.
Anderton, 145.
Andrews, 151.
Anger, 117.
Aristoxenus, 22, 25.
Armes, *106*, 108.
Arne, *87*. 45
Arnold, G. B., *106*, 107.
Arnold, S., *91*, 90, 138.
Artizans made B.A. and M.A., 41.
Arts, Faculty of, 15.
Ashbroke, 12.
Asquith, 147.
Atkins, F. P., 107.
Atkins, J., 119.
Atkins, J. A., 118.
Atkinson, 145.
Attwood, 141, 147.

Aumusse, 57.
Aylward, 94.
Ayrton, 93, *137*, 139.

Baccalauriat, 8.
Bachelor, derivation of word, 10.
—— of Arts, 9, 10, 42, 60.
—— of Grammar. See Grammar Degrees.
—— of Music, 15, 17, 21, 42, 60, 61.
—— Fees for, 14.
—— no special dress for, 60.
Baker, G., 97.
Baker, H., 109.
Bambridge, 111.
Bangcrofte, 125.
Banister, 49.
Banks, 142.
Barker, 75.
Barkworth, 117.
Barnard, 110.
Barratt, 113.
Barrett, 110.
Barrow, 149.
Bartlett, 76.
Bateman, 116.
Bates, 54, 140.
Bather, 112.
Bathing, 14.
Batson, 113.
Battishill, 138.
Beckwith, 98.
Beecroft, 109.
Beeston, 132.
Beethoven, 140.
Belcher, *109*, 111.
Bellamy, 137.
Bellerby, 114.
Benet, 13.
Bengough, 111.
Bennett, A., *100*, 101.
Bennett, G. J., *150*, 151.

Bennett, J., 132.
Bennett, W. S., 38, 56, 105, 110, *143*, 146.
Benson, 147.
Bentlee, 46.
Bentley, F., 114.
Bentley, J. M., *147*, 148.
Berry, 151.
Beryderyke, 18, *122*, 155.
Beryngton, 45.
Berytus, 7.
Bexfield, *104*, 142.
Bianchi, 102.
Binchois, 13.
Birch, 112.
Bird, 46, 72, 73, 76, 123.
Biretta, 59.
Bishop, 36, 101, *102*, 105, 106.
Blair, 150.
Blitheman, 71, *124*.
Bliss, 108.
Blow, 83, 84, 131.
Blyth, 101.
Board of Musical Studies, 39, 42, 44.
Bodleian Library, 32.
Boethius, 18, 20, 21, 65, 67.
Boissier, 113.
Boito, 151.
Bologna, 7, 8, 13.
Borow. See Burrow.
Boyce, 86, 133, *134*, 136.
Boyse, 75.
Bradbury, 111.
Bradfield, 117.
Bradford, *111*, 114.
Bradley, 112.
Brett, 127.
Bridge, J. C., *112*, 116.
Bridge, J. F., *109*, 112.
Bridgetower, 139.
Briggs, *148*, 149.
Brightwyn, 68.
Brind, 132.
Brooksbank, 111.
Brown, *113*, 115.
Bruch, 151.
Buck, P. C., 118.
Buck, Z., 104, 106.
Bucknall, 113.
Bulgarus, 7.
Bull, 17, 46, *71*, 74.
Bunnett, *144*, 145.
Burney, *90*, 137.
Burrow, 122.
Bursar's book, 53.
Busby, 138.
Bussell, 118.

Buswell, 88, *135*.
Buttons, 60.
Byrchynshaw, 12.

Caldicott, 147.
Callcott, *93*, 98.
Cambridge University, 11.
—— Ceremonies, 61, 62.
—— Dress for Graduates in Music, 60, 61.
—— Music at, 53, 56.
—— New Regulations of, 1893, 43.
Camden, 78, 125.
Camidge, *140*, 141.
Canterbury Degrees, 10, *note*.
Carleton. } See Charlton.
Carlton. }
Carling, 111.
Carnaby, 139.
Carnall, 146.
Carnell, 114.
Carr, 115, 118, *149*.
Ceremonies, 10, 61, 62.
Chambers, *148*, 150.
Chaperon, 57.
Chard, 140.
Charde, 67.
Charlton, 124.
Chaundy, 117.
Chell, 67.
Child, *80*, 82.
Chipp, *144*, 145.
Choirs dispersed, 47.
Choppinus, 10.
Choragus, 35-37.
Clark, F. S., 109.
Clark, Jeremiah, 84.
Clarke, F. W., 114.
Clarke, J. H. S., 109.
Clarke, Jeremiah, 97.
Clarke-Whitfeld, 38, 61, *95*, 100, 138, 141.
Clawsey, 66.
Claxton, 115.
Clerks, 20.
Cliffe, F. H., 118.
Cock, 74, 125.
Cockle, 115.
Colborne, 145.
Coleman, 128.
Collard, 79.
Collinson, 113.
Colman. See Coleman.
Communion Service in place of Mass, 19.
Concentores Sodales, 97, 98.
Concerts, 27, 32, 39, 51-56.

INDEX.   161

Constantinople, 7.
Cook, Captain, 128, 131.
Cooke, B., 136.
Cooper, Master J., 45.
Cooper, Robert, 16, *121*, 154.
Coper. See Cooper (Robert).
Corbett, *146*, 148.
Corfe, 36, 37, 52, *104*, 106.
Corke, 151.
Cornets, 50.
Coryphæus, 36, 37.
Coward, 117.
Cowper. See Cooper (Robert).
Cox, 151.
Coy, *113*, 116.
Craddock, 111.
Crament, 114,
Creser, *110*, 114.
Crewe, Lord, 35.
Croft, 83, *84*, 132, 136.
Crook, 148.
Crosse, 122.
Crotch, 36, 37, *96*, 98, 100, 101, 102, 138, 143.
Crow, *146*, 148.
Crowe, *145*, 146.
Cruickshank, 116.
Cutler, 100.
Curtseys, 47.

Dale, A. S., 117.
Dale, R. F., 108.
Daniel, 76.
Darby, 149.
Davies, H., 79.
Davies, H. W., 151.
Dawber, 147.
Dawke, 66.
Deane, 86.
Dearle, 142.
Deering. See Dering.
Degrees: A license to teach, 8.
—— given by Pope, 9.
—— Canterbury, 10.
—— in single arts, 12, 13.
—— accumulation of, 17.
—— in music omitted from registers, 64.
—— earliest recorded degree in music at Oxford, 66.
—— earliest recorded degree in music at Cambridge, 15.
Dering, 77.
Dewberry, F., 149.
Dewberry, W. C., 150.
D'Ewes, 28.
Disputations, 19, 40, 41.

Dixon, G., *106*, 107.
Doctor, Degree of, 7,'8, 9.
—— title of, 11, 17.
—— of Music, 15, 18.
Doctorate conferred without Baccalauriat, 17, 42.
Doctors of Music men of eminence, 17.
—— not connected with University as teachers, 17.
—— no special dress for, 60, 61.
—— Cope to be worn by, 61.
Dodds, *112*, 116.
Dowland, 73.
Draper, 19, *67*.
Dress, Regulation of, 59, 60.
Dufay, 13.
Dunstable, 13, 14.
Dunstan, *148*, 151.
Dupuis, *94*.
Dvorák, 151.
Dyer, *111*, 114.
Dygon, 66.

East, 126.
Eccles, 133.
Ede, *65*.
Edwards, A. C., 117.
Edwards, H. J., *112*, 116.
Ellis, 47, *81*.
Elizabeth, Reign of, 46.
Elvey, G. J., *101*, 103.
Elvey, S., 36, *101*.
Emery, 115.
Emmot, or Emot, 78.
English School of Music, 13.
Erasmus, 14.
Essex, *99*, 100.
Est, Este. See East.
Eugene III., Pope, 8.
Eusden, 31.
Eveleigh, Dr., 40.
Eveleigh, W. G., 117.
Examinations, 19, 39, 40, 41, 143.
Exercise, 26-29, 32, 38, 41, 42, 62.

Faculty, 15.
Fall, 148.
Fairfax, 16, 66, *120*, 154.
Farmer, 130.
Farnaby, 73.
Farrell, 150.
Fawcett, 105.
Feasts, 61.
Fees, 14, 58, 63.
Ferfax. See Fairfax.
Ferrabosco, 129.
Field, 116.

L

Firtun, 19, *122*, 154.
Fisher, C. W., 149.
Fisher, H., *147*, 148.
Fisher, J. A., 92.
Flowers, *103*, 108.
Floyd, 152.
Forest, 13.
Frevill. See Fryvill.
Frith, 79.
Frost, *147*, 148.
Fryvill, 17, 18, *120*, 121, 153, 154.
Frye, 150.
Fuller, 132.
Fytz-John, 45.

Gaisford Dean, 48.
Galileo, 23.
Gale, 117.
Gardner, 112.
Garland, 113.
Garrett, 39, *144*, 145.
Gates, 91, 94, 133, 135.
Gaul, 145.
Gervasius, 14.
Gibbons, C., 28, 80, *82*.
Gibbons, E., 74.
Gibbons, O., 60, 74, 78, 79, *125*, 156.
Gilbert, J., 66.
Gilbert, W. B., *106*, 117.
Giles, 19, *70*, 79, 80.
Gladstone, *147*, 148.
Glexney, 47.
Gloves, 58, 62, 63, 79.
Godwin, 70.
Goodban, 104.
Goodhart, 151.
Goodman, *65*.
Goodson, R., Sen., 36, *83*.
—— Jun., 36, *85*.
Goss, 110, *147*.
Gower, *112*, 115.
Gowns, 57, 60, 61.
Graduates' Meeting, 91, 94, 136, 157.
Graff, 93.
Grammar Degrees, 12, 13, 14, 17, 63.
—— Schools, 12.
—— Faculty of, 15.
Gratianus, 8.
Gray, *149*, 150.
Greene, 32, 38, 85, 87, *132*, 134, 135.
Greenish, A. J., *149*, 151.
Greenish, F. R., *115*, 118.
Gregory IX., 10.
Gregory, G. H., 111.
Greig, *113*, 117.
Grieg, 151.
Grosvenor, 105.

Gaudeloupe, F. de, 118.
Guarnerius. See Irnerius.
Guinneth, 16, *68*.
Guise, 135.
Gwyn, 31.
Gwyneth. See Guinneth.

Habyngton. See Abyngton.
Hackett, 105.
Hadow, 117.
Hague, 28, *138*.
Haking, *106*, 108.
Halton, 148.
Hamboys, 15, 152.
Hamilton, 109.
Hamm, 72.
Hancock, 111.
Handel, 29, 132.
Hannaford, 150.
Harding, *113*, 115.
Harpsichords, 54.
Harris, 101.
Hartmann, 112.
Harwood, 114.
Hatherley, 106.
Hattersley, 150.
Hauptmann, 143.
Hawes, 101, 144.
Hawley, 132.
Hawkins, 132.
Haydn, 94.
Hayes, P., 32, 36, *89*, 92, 96, 98.
Hayes, W., 36, *86*, 87, 98.
Hayne, 37, *106*, 107.
Healey, 111.
Heap, *145*, 146.
Heather, 59, 70, 74, *78*.
—— Lectureship, &c., 31, 32, 35, 79.
Heighington, 152.
Hele, 111.
Hellendaal, 138.
Helmore, 52.
Hemmings, 116.
Hempel, *106*, 107.
Herbert, 107.
Heyther. See Heather.
Hewlett, 108.
Hibbert, N. B., 118.
Higgs, 111.
High Mass, 20.
Hiles, *107*, 109.
Hill, *145*, 148.
Hilton, 46, *127*.
Hindle, 95.
Hine, 86.
Hodges, 141.
Holder, 95.

INDEX.

Holloway, 112.
Holmes, 143.
Honorary Degrees, 114.
Hood, 57-59, 61.
Hopkins, J. L., *142*, 145.
Hopper, 150.
Hornpipe, 45.
Horsley, 98.
Hosear, 45.
Howard, 136.
Hudson, 137.
Huges de Malmecestre, 11.
Hugolinus, 7.
Hulton, 109.
Humfrey, 131.
Hummel, 140.
Humphrey, Duke, 34, 157.
Hunt, H. G. B., 112.
Hunt, T., 153.
Huntley, 150.
Hutchinson, 114.

Iliffe, *111*, 114.
Inceptor, 14, 27.
Ingelo, 28.
Inventories, Fifteenth Century, 45.
I'ons, *104*, 106.
Irnerius, 7.
Isham, or Isum, *83*, 84.
Ives, 149.

Jackson, Bass-Violist, 47.
Jackson, W., 139.
Jackson, W. F. W., 113.
Janys, 67.
James, 149.
James, Vice-Chancellor, 38.
Jay, 140.
Jefferies, or Jeffrye, 74.
Jenkins, 147.
Joachim, 147.
Johnson, E., 124.
Johnson, T., 150.
Jolley, 116.
Jones, J. J., 100.
Jones, R., 75.
Jordan, *110*.
Jowett, 118.
Joyner, 12.
Justinian, 7.

Karn, 149.
Keeton, *110*, 113.
Kelway, 134.
Kemp, 139.
Kennedy, A., 118.
Kilburn, 148.

King, A., *111*, 117.
King, C., *83*, 87, 132, 134.
King, R., 131.
Kirby, 46.
Kiss, part of the Ceremonial in conferring Doctorate of Music, 62, *note*.
Knyvett, 138, 147.
Koeller, 116.
Kunz, 117.

Lake, 78.
Lamb, 115.
Langdon, 88.
Langran, 115.
Lant, 157.
Lateran Council, 9.
Latham, 148.
Lawrence, 112.
Law, Faculty of, 15.
Lawes, H., 128.
Lawson, 147.
Leaver, 149.
Lectures, 30, 31, 34, 35, 38, 39, 42.
Lee, 149.
Leeds, 150.
Lessy, 18, *120*, 153.
Lewis, 116.
Liberal Arts, 11, 32, 34.
Licentiate, 8, 9.
Liddle, 147.
Lillingston, 116.
Lister, 112.
Little, *113*, 116.
Littledale, 101.
Lloyd, C. F., 113.
Lloyd, C. H., 52, *110*, 118.
Locke, 74, 128.
Lomas, 112.
Lombard, Peter, 8.
Long, B., 104.
Long, Roger, 32, 55.
Loosemore, G., 129.
Loosemoore, H., 53, *128*.
Lotharius, 7.
Lott, 112.
Lowe, 28, 36, 47, 50, 131.
Lugge, 81.
Lydberg, 45.

Macfarren, 38, 114, *146*.
Macleane, *107*, 108.
Mackenzie, 150.
Magistri Musicales, 13
Malmène, 145.
Manini, 138.
Mann, *111*, 115.

L 2

Marbeck, *69*, 72.
Marchant, 114.
Marks, J. C., *108*, 110.
Marks, T. O., 110.
Marsden, *147*.
Marshall, *101*, 103.
Marson, 152.
Martin, 7.
Martin, G. C., 109.
Martyn, 116.
Mason, 65.
Master of Arts, 9, 11, 12, 15, 20, 30, 31.
—— of Music, 29, 44, 48, 79.
—— Title of, 8, 9.
Mathews, 141.
Matriculation, 43.
Matthew, of Paris, 9.
Mayo, 150.
MacMurdie, 100.
Meacham, 145.
Medicine, Degrees in, 7.
—— Faculty of, 15.
Mee, 37, *115*, 117.
Meers, 113.
Mendelssohn, 98, 142, 143.
Mendus or Mend, 68.
Merbecke. See Marbeck.
Merrick, 108.
Merriken, 115.
Middleton, *149*, 150.
Millar, 70.
Miller, E., 137.
Miller, G. J., 151.
Miller, H. W., 108.
Mills, 115.
Mitchell, 113.
Modena, 13.
Monk, E. G., 52, *104*.
Monk, M. J., *113*, 117.
Moore, 116.
Morley, F. W., 149.
Morley, T., *72*.
Morley, W., 84.
Müller, 111.
Munday, *72*, 79.
Music Act, 21, 27-29, 61.
—— Lecture, or Speech, 28, 30-32.
—— School, 28, 31, 32, 35, 48.
—— one of the subjects for degree of M.A., 20.
—— Time of study, 20, 40.
—— Cultivation of, 45, 47.
—— at Cambridge, 53-56.
—— at Oxford, 47-51.
—— suppressed, 47.
—— room, 50.
—— not a faculty, 15, 34.

Myerscough, 115.

Naylor, C. L., 151.
Naylor, E. W., 151.
Naylor, J., *107*, 111.
Nares, 91, 95, *135*, 137, 139.
Netherlands School, 14.
Newboult, 150.
Nichol, 116.
Nichols, 148.
Nicholson, 36, *74*.
Nixon, 147.
Norris, *89*, 96.
Northbrooke, 68.
Nunn, 145.

Oakeley, *114*, 145.
Oakey, 147.
Odoacer, 21.
O'Donaghue, 108.
Oelrichs, 3.
Okeover, 81.
Organs, 16, 46-50, 52-54.
Ouseley, 36, 37, 41, *105*, 106 107.
Owen, 108.
Oxford, University of, 11.
—— Musical Societies at, 52.
Oysters, 62.

Pacey, 111.
Packer, 48.
Padua, 40.
Palmer, C. C., 118.
Palmer, E. D., 113.
Palmer, T., 114.
Paris, University of, 8, 9.
—— Disturbances at, 9.
Parker, H., 18, *65*.
Parker, J., 121, 154.
Parratt, 52, *111*.
Parry, C. H. H., 36, *109*, 115, 149.
Parry, J., *145*, 148.
Pattinson, 148.
Payne, 152.
Peace, *110*, 112.
Peacock, 117.
Pearce, C. W., *148*, 149.
Pearce, S. A., *107*, 108.
Pearce, S. J., 107.
Pearson, M., 77.
Peel, 111.
Pen, 67.
Pepusch, *85*, 134, 135, 136.
Perrot, 16, 19, *66*, 121.
Person. See Pearson.
Petch, 106.
Peterson, 118.

Petre, 67
Philipps, 36, *81*.
Piers, 58, 78.
Pierson. See Pearson.
Piggott, F., 84, *131*, 135.
Piggott, H., 150.
Pileus, 7, 59.
Pilkington, 74.
Pinney, 112.
Plainsong, 21.
Plant, 115.
Plummer, 122.
Plumridge, *111*, 117.
Pole, *107*, 109.
Porret. See Perrot.
Porter, 75.
Potter, 143.
Powel, 29.
Power, 13.
Prælector publicus in Musica, 31, 157.
Precentor, 36.
Price, 116.
Priest, H., 111.
Priest, W. J., 110.
Pring, Isaac, 97.
Pring, Jacob C., 97.
Pring, Joseph, 99.
Pringuer, *113*, 116.
Prior, *107*, 113.
Professor of Music, Duties of, 37, 39.
—— Election of, 38.
—— Dress of, 61.
—— Lists of, 36, 38.
Professorship of Music, 34.
—— Foundation of, at Cambridge, 130.
Propert, 105.
Ptolemæus, 22.
Pugh, 116.
Purcell, D., 132.
Purcell, H., 130.
Puritans, 49.
Pye, J. T., 113.
Pye, K. J., 104.
Pypis, 120.
Pythagoras, 22, 23.

Quadrivium, 9, 10, 11, 30.
Quarles, 131.
Questionists, 62,
Quin, 48.

Radcliffe Library, 33.
Ramsey, 60, *127*, 156.
Randall, 38, 54, 61, 96, *133*, 135, 138.
Ravenscroft, J., 125, *note*.
Ravenscroft, T., 126.
Read, *112*, 118.

Reade, 74.
Reading, 85.
Reay, 111.
Redhead, 104.
Regals, Tuner of, 84.
Regent-Masters, 34.
Requirements for Degrees, 16, 18, 21, 40, 41, 43.
Revell, 116.
Reynolds, 117.
Richardson, 116.
Richter, 116.
Righton, 115.
Ringrose, 110.
Riseley, 112.
Robert the Harpmaker, 45.
Roberts, J. H., 148.
Roberts, J. V., 52, *111*, 113.
Robertson, 149.
Robinson, G. H., 149.
Robinson, Org. of Westminster Abbey, 136.
Rogers, L. J., 115.
Rogers, B., 80, 83, *128*.
Rogers, R., *110*, 112.
Roman Law, 7.
Romberg, 13, *note*.
Rome, 7.
Roper, 149.
Royle, 118.
Russell, J., *107*, 108.
Russell, W., Mus. B., 1808, *99*, 100.
Russell, W., Mus. B., 1865, 108.
Russell, W. A. B., 117.
Ryley, 118.

Saint-Saëns, 151.
Saintwix, or Saint Just, 15, *119*, 153.
Salerno, 7.
Sampson, 112.
Sandwich, Lord, 54.
Sangster, *110*, 113.
Sankey, 107.
Saunders, *111*, 114.
Savilian Professors, 27, 36.
Sawyer, F. J., *113*, 115.
Sawyer, T., 31.
Scherman, 65.
Scholar in Music, 34.
Scholastical Musitians, 48.
Schools Quadrangle, 32.
Scrope, S. le, 59.
Seal, 114.
Seven Liberal Arts, 9, 11, 32.
Sewell, 104.
Shepeard, or Sheppard, 46, *69*.
Shinn, 148.

Sidebotham, 114.
Simpson, 116.
Sims, 113.
Simms, 111.
Singing taught, 20.
Sloman, *107*, 109.
Smith, A. F., 149.
Smith, C., *95*, 98.
Smith, G. H., 113.
Smith, J. S., 101.
Smith, Dr. R., 54.
Smith, T., 117.
Sneddon, 149.
Snow, 131.
Southward, 150.
Speer, 150.
Spinets, 54.
Spinney, 108.
Spohr, 143.
Staggins, 37, 38, *130*, 156.
Stainer, 36, 52, *107*, 108.
Stamps, 117.
Stanford, 38, 115, *150*.
Stanistreet, 107.
Stanley, *85*, 87.
Stark, 112.
Statutes of Cambridge, 1559, 14.
—— of Clare, 1359, 20.
—— of Oxford, 1356, 15, 20; 1431, 20; (of Laud), 1636, 14 *note*, 17, 27, 35, 39, 61; 1769, 60; 1856, 37.
Steggall, 142.
Stephens, 136.
Stephenson. See Stevenson, R.
Stevens, A. H., 115.
Stevens, H., 148.
Stevenson, R., 17, *72*, 75.
Stevenson, W. E., 117.
Stewart, 41, 105.
Stimpson, 111.
Stokes, 148.
Stokoe, 148.
Stonard, 76.
Stone, 114.
Storer, 113.
Stowe, 13.
Such, 147.
Sullivan, 114, *147*.
Summers, 116.
Sweeting, 117.
Sylvester, 67.
Synge, 108.

Tallis, 46, 123.
Taylor, E. W., *113*, 115.
Taylor, H., 151.

Taylor, James, 52, 111.
Taylor, John, M.A., 32.
Taylor, John, Mus.B., 148.
Taylor, Sedley, 39.
Taylor, Sylvanus, 29.
Taylor, T., 68.
Taylor, W., 106.
Tearne, 114.
Tena, 59.
Tendall, 111.
Terry, 56.
Thackeray, 110.
Theodoric, 22.
Theology, 8, 10.
Thieves given degrees, 41.
Thomas, W. E., 117, 118.
Thomason, 113.
Thompson, 109.
Thomson, 136.
Tiley, *108*, 112.
Tireman, 54, *135*.
Tomkins, J., 77, *126*, 156.
Tomkins, T., *76*, 126.
Tozer, 118.
Travers, 94.
Trebatius, 9.
Trego, 113.
Trembath, 110.
Trent, Archives of, 13.
Trimnell, 112.
Trivium, 9, 10, 11.
Troman, 112.
Trotter *116*, 118.
Tschaikowsky, 151.
Tudway, 38, 60, *129*, 132, 133.
Turle, 142.
Turner, J. B., 145.
Turner, R. H., 151.
Turner, W., 131.
Turpin, 148.
Tutt, 148.
Tye, 17, 19, 60, 69, *122*, 155.

Uffenbach, 53.

Vauler, 78,
Van, 45.
Verrinder, 107.
Vesperies, 35.
Vicary, 99.
Vincent, *113*, 116.
Vinning, 148.

Wainwright, 92.
Waits, 125.
Wale, 111.
Walker, E,, 118.

INDEX.

Walker, L., 151.
Walmisley, 38, *141*, 142, 134.
Walond, 87.
Walter, 114.
Walton, 111.
Wanless, 131.
Wanley, 53.
Ward, 112.
Wareing, *148*, 149.
Warren, 145.
Washington, 151.
Waterhouse, 74.
Watkins, 19, *121*, 154.
Watson, E., 12.
Watson, H., *148*, 150.
Watts, 149.
Weale, 132.
Webb, 95.
Webber, 117.
Wedow. See Wydow.
Weelkes, 46, *75*.
Weekes, 146.
Wendon, 19, *66*.
Wernerius. See Irnerius.
Wesley, 103.
Westbrook, *147*, 148.
Wever, 127.
Whatmoor, 151.
Wheeldon, 150.
Whinfield, 117.
White, M., 80.
White, R., 46, *123*, 155.
Whyte, J., 68.
Whytt. See White, R.
Wigthorpe, 76,

Wilbye, 46.
Williams, A., 118.
Williams, C. F. A., 117, *151*.
Williams, C. L., 113.
Williams, S. H., 110.
Willoughby, 118.
Wilson, A. W., 118.
Wilson, D. F., 116.
Wilson, J., 28, 36, 47, *82*.
Wilson, R. H., 112.
Winn, *112*, 115.
Wise, 150.
Wiseman, 150.
Wodde, 66.
Wolstenholme, 116.
Wood, A., 18, 28.
Wood, C., 150.
Wood, D. J., 112.
Woodcock, 99.
Woodroffe, 132.
Woods, 118.
Woodward, 108.
Worgan, *134*, 136.
Wright, 113.
Wrigley, J. G., 114.
Wrigley, W. A., 115.
Wydow, 60, 65, 119, *121*, 154.
Wylde, H., 142.
Wylde, J., 14.

Ximines, 54.

Young, 67.

Zacharias, 14.

For EU product safety concerns, contact us at Calle de José Abascal, 56–1°,
28003 Madrid, Spain or eugpsr@cambridge.org.

www.ingramcontent.com/pod-product-compliance
Ingram Content Group UK Ltd.
Pitfield, Milton Keynes, MK11 3LW, UK
UKHW041418180426
11947UKWH00007B/194